DAVID BAKER'S
ARRANGING & COMPOSING

For the Small Ensemble:
Jazz, R&B, Jazz-Rock

REVISED EDITION

D1599503

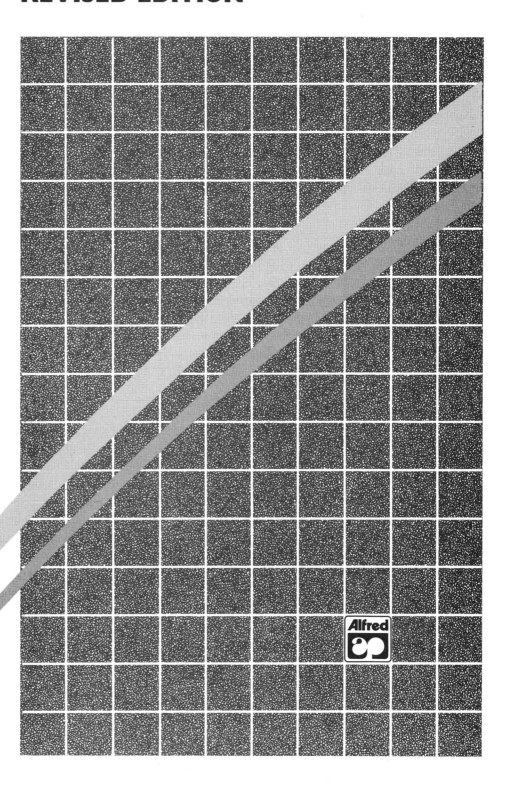

Alfred

Revised Edition

© Copyright MCMLXXXV by Frangipani Press
© Copyright assigned MCMLXXXVIII Alfred Publishing Co., Inc.

All Rights Reserved
Print in the United States of America

ISBN 0-88284-469-5

Table of Contents

Biographical Notes iv

Foreword by Quincy Jones v

Preface vi

Chapter I: Nomenclature 1

Chapter II: The Instruments 6

Chapter III: General Rules for Instrumental Scoring 12

Chapter IV: Constructing a Melody 16

Chapter V: Techniques To Be Used in Developing a Melody 20

Chapter VI: Fitting Chords To a Given Melodic Line 45

Chapter VII: Writing for the Rhythm Section 52

Chapter VIII: The Piano Trio . . . .·.. 56

Chapter IX: The Jazz Quartet 59

Chapter X: Scales and Their Relationship To Chords 60

Chapter XI: Two-Voice Writing 77

Chapter XII: Turnbacks 90

Chapter XIII: Three-Voice Writing 93

Chapter XIV: Four-Voice Writing 101

Chapter XV: Five-Voice Writing 113

Chapter XVI: Six-Voice Writing 123

Chapter XVII: Bitonal Writing 125

Chapter XVIII: Putting an Arrangement Together 135

Chapter XIX: Chord Substitutions 139

Chapter XX: The Blues and Rhythm & Blues 145

Chapter XXI: A Model Arrangement 153

 Alfred has made every effort to make this book not only attractive but more useful and long-lasting as well. Usually, large books do not lie flat or stay open on the music rack. In addition, the pages (which are glued together) tend to break away from the spine after repeated use.

In this edition, pages are sewn together in multiples of 16. This special process prevents pages from falling out of the book while allowing it to stay open for ease in playing. We hope this unique binding will give you added pleasure and additional use.

Biographical Notes

DAVID NATHANIEL BAKER—author, composer, arranger, instrumentalist, and teacher—is a gifted and versatile musician equally at home in all worlds of music.

Born December 21, 1931 in Indianapolis, Indiana, Baker first established his musical reputation as a brilliant jazz trombonist. He worked with the big bands of Stan Kenton, Maynard Ferguson, Buddy Johnson, Lionel Hampton, and Quincy Jones and with combos led by Wes Montgomery, Harold Land, Charles Tyler, and most notably, George Russell. Currently, Baker performs on cello.

Baker holds the B.M.E. and M.M.E. degrees from Indiana University. He studied trombone with Thomas Beversdorf, William Adam, J. J. Johnson, Bob Brookmeyer, and others; cello with Leopold Teraspulsky, Jules Eskin, Norma Woodbury, Helga Winold, Janos Starker, and others; and theory and composition with George Russell, William Russo, John Lewis, Gunther Schuller, Bernard Heiden, and others.

Baker received a *down beat* Hall of Fame Scholarship Award in 1959 and won *down beat's* New Star Award: Trombone in the 1962 International Jazz Critics Poll. In 1981 he was the recipient of the National Association of Jazz Educators Hall of Fame Award.

In the non-jazz realm Baker has been a member of the Indiana University Philharmonic and Opera orchestras and the Wind and Brass Ensemble; the Butler University Orchestra, Band, and Brass Ensemble; and the Indianapolis Civic Orchestra. He has made solo appearances with and has had his compositions performed by the New York Philharmonic, among many orchestras. Artists who have performed Baker's compositions include Josef Gingold, Janos Starker, Ruggerio Ricci, James Pellerite, Gary Karr, Bertram Turetzky, and Harvey Phillips.

David Baker is currently Professor of Music at the Indiana University School of Music and is Chairman of the Jazz Department, supervising one of the most important jazz studies programs in the U.S. He also travels extensively in his various roles as clinician, lecturer, performer, and conductor.

Foreword

David Baker is one of those rare people who has everything covered. He's a total musician. I mean, Bartok to Boogaloo. In this book, he gets into piano trios, jazz quartets; he explores four and five-voice writing, chord substitutions, rhythm & blues voicings and bass patterns, and a whole lot of other mind-stretchers.

I was privileged to have Dave in my big band in 1961, as a trombonist, bass trombonist, arranger and composer. He had (and has) a stimulating, provocative kind of mind plus a roaring sense of humor. He was a prober, always curious about everything, life and music. But at the same time, he was stable. He was someone you could count on when everything was going crazy, which was nearly always. Freddie Hubbard was in the band then too, and David Baker was his music teacher in Indianapolis.

This book is an intensive study. It covers far more than its title implies, including as it does many of Dave's original compositions. I'm a big fan of Dave's writing. I remember a tune he brought with him when he joined my band. It was called *Screamin' Meemies*. Since then the tune has become a standard with bands all over the country, large and small, especially school jazz bands. As a matter of fact, David Baker's musical influence is strongly felt on campuses from one coast to the other.

I'd like to add that David Baker has been almost a pioneer in collating information on the histories of black composers in America.

I'd also like to go on record with the reason I was late in submitting this foreword to the publisher. When I sat down to write it, I got all hung up in the book instead. And that's just what you should do too, if you're a writer, or if you're thinking about becoming one. This book is a great trip through the working foundations of modern music.

Quincy Jones

Preface

This book addresses itself to the needs of the composer-arranger who is interested in writing for small combinations (3–10 pieces) in jazz, rhythm & blues, and jazz-rock. Many books have been written across the years dealing with jazz band arranging and/or composing but almost without exception these books have concerned themselves primarily with the exigencies of large ensemble writing. I suppose that much of the neglect in this area has been the result of the mistaken notion that writing for small groups does not require the skills and disciplines necessary for big band writing. The situation is much like the ignorance that so long inhibited the teaching of jazz improvisation. This lack of knowledge manifested itself in attitudes such as "you either got it or you ain't".

In many ways the writing for small combination is much more difficult than writing for the big band. In big bands, with complete sections of brass and saxophones, the task of combining orchestral colors is much less precarious. Certain aspects of composition and arranging can be treated much more loosely in the context of the big band. Such problems as creating the illusion of a brass section when you have two brass and three reeds, or getting a full chord sound with only three instruments, or achieving contrast and variety with limited tonal resources, are problems usually endemic to small group writing.

Learning to write for small groups is particularly valuable for many reasons, musical and non-musical. Although the big band continues to be the ideal toward which aspiring composer-arrangers strive, it is easier to organize a six to nine-piece ensemble than a twenty-piece big band. Another reason is, of course, the popularity of the small ensemble in contemporary jazz, rhythm & blues, and jazz-rock. Even within the context of a large ensemble, small ensembles offer welcome relief in terms of contrast and variety. From the standpoint of economics the small group is more likely to get work than the big band. From an aesthetic point of view most innovations and departures from tradition have taken place within the smaller ensemble. The unwieldiness of large ensembles, the relatively strict adherence to established big band practices, and the traditional role of the big band as synthesizer have all contributed to this state of affairs. For these and other reasons, many young writers will want to explore the area of small group writing.

This book includes excerpts from small group arrangements, complete scores of recorded and published arrangements, musical examples, recommended recordings, and suggested outside reading. The book also provides many of the compositional tools for the arranger, for all good arrangers must be able to compose or forever remain mediocre in their writing efforts. Often the composing will be simply writing introductions, interludes, countermelodies, etc., but in every sense of the word, composing.

Simply put, it is the purpose of this book to make available the techniques for developing skills necessary to a composer-arranger (or teacher) in writing for small groups.

David Baker
Bloomington, Indiana
January, 1985

Chapter I

NOMENCLATURE

One of the first things that an aspiring jazz musician must do is learn to read and interpret chord symbols. The six chord types are major, minor, dominant, diminished, augmented, and half diminished.

An alphabetical letter indicates the root on which a chord is built. The tertian system is usually employed, that is, chords are built in consecutive thirds (i.e., C-E-G-B-D-F-A). For the uninitiated two short cuts to aid in chord construction follow: (1) build the chord using alternating letters of the musical alphabet (i.e., F-A-C-E-G-B-D-etc.) and (2) build the chord using either the lines E-G-B-D-F or the spaces F-A-C-E.

In the major chord types all notes are indigenous to the major scale of the root tone, i.e. C major is spelled C-E-G-B-D-etc., Eb major is spelled Eb-G-Bb-D-F-etc., and so forth. Numerically this can be expressed 1-3-5-7-9-11-etc. A letter standing alone usually indicates a major triad, which is a chord consisting of the root, the major third, and the perfect fifth, i.e., C-E-G, F-A-C, Gb-Bb-Db, etc.

All major type chords have the word "major" or one of the symbols of abbreviation in the title with the exception of the triad (i.e., C-E-G) and the chord of the added sixth (i.e., C_6=C-E-G-A). The term extension refers to the notes higher than the seventh in a tertian structure, i.e., the ninth, eleventh, thirteenth, etc. We may extend the major chord by using the letter names of the major scale built on the root of the chord (i.e., Ab major 13, which is spelled Ab-C-Eb-G-Bb-Db-F) or by using the unaltered odd numbers (1-3-5-7-9-11-13). The most commonly used symbols and abbreviations for major are Maj, Ma, M, $\triangle$, a letter by itself, and a letter plus the number six, i.e., the following: C Maj, C Ma, C M, C $\triangle$, C, and C_6. In abbreviations for major use a capital letter M for the first letter of the abbreviation.

All minor type chords have the word minor (use small letter m) or one of the symbols or abbreviations for minor in the title with the exception of the half diminished chord. For our purposes the half diminished chord is better called a minor seventh with a flat five ($mi_7^{(b5)}$). The most commonly used symbols and abbreviations for minor are min, mi, m, and –, i.e., the following: C min, C mi, C m, and C–. To this we may add the numbers which indicate the members of the scale to be added, i.e., C mi 11, which is spelled C-Eb-G-Bb-D-F.

In constructing a minor chord we again think of the root of the chord as being the tonic note of a major scale. We then lower the third of the chord one half step. The resultant triad is indicated by a letter plus the word minor or one of its abbreviations. To this triad we may add the lowered or minor seventh. The spelling is then 1-b3-5-b7; if we use the note C as the root of the chord, $C mi_7$ is spelled C-Eb-G-Bb. Any extensions added to the minor chord are indigenous to the major scale of the root tone; C mi 11 is spelled, for example, C-Eb-G-Bb-D-F or 1-b3-5-b7-9-11.

An altered chord tone or extension is indicated by a plus (+) or sharp (#) for raised and by a minus (–) or flat (b) for lowered. Altered and added notes are best parenthesized to avoid confusion, i.e., $C_7^{(b9)}$, $C_7^{(add\ 4)}$, and $Cmi_7^{(b9)}$.

The dominant seventh chord is constructed as follows: 1-3-5-b7, or, in other words, lower the seventh of the major scale of the root one half step (using C as the root, the chord is spelled C-E-G-Bb). The number seven, unless accompanied by the word major or minor, means to add the minor seventh to the triad. Any letter plus a number other than six signifies a dominant seventh chord, i.e. the following: C_9 is spelled C-E-G-Bb-D; C_{13} is spelled C-E-G-Bb-D-F-A. All extensions are indigenous to the major key of the root tone, i.e. the following: C_{13} is spelled C-E-G-Bb-D-F-A.

The diminished chord is constructed 1-b3-b5-6; using C as the root the chord is spelled C-Eb-Gb-A. In jazz all references to a diminished chord mean diminished seventh. In this chord all adjacent members are a minor third apart. The symbol for diminished is a circle; its abbreviation is dim. (small letter d).

The augmented chord is constructed 1-3-#5; using C as the root the chord is spelled C-E-G#. In this chord all adjacent members are a major third apart. The symbol for augmented is a plus sign (+); its abbreviation is aug.

The half diminished chord is also known as a minor seventh with a flat five ($mi_7^{(b5)}$) and is constructed 1-b3-b5-b7; using C as the root the chord is spelled C-Eb-Gb-Bb. The half diminished chord is symbolized ø and abbreviated $mi_7^{(b5)}$.

All chords that are neither major nor minor function as dominant seventh chords, i.e., C+, C_{13}, Co_7, C_{11}, etc. The augmented chord usually functions as the dominant seventh chord with the same root name, i.e., C+=C_7(+5). Diminished chords are usually derived dominant seventh chords. The root tone is found a major third below the bottom tone of the diminished chord, i.e. Co_7=Ab_7.

One of the most perplexing problems for beginning jazz players is reconciling the key signature of a composition to the seeming inconsistencies in the realizations of the chord symbols, i.e., the following examples:

Why is there no Eb in this chord?

Why is there no F# in this chord?

In answering these questions observe the following rule: the key signature of a composition has no direct bearing on the spelling of individual chords. The symbols dictate the realization of the chord.

Properly interpreting the chord of the added sixth poses another problem for many people because this chord is often an inverted form of a minor seventh chord. This problem should be handled as follows: if the chord of the added sixth resolves to a dominant seventh chord a major second above or a dominant seventh chord a major third below its root, it should be treated as a minor seventh chord. To locate its root, invert the chord until it is arranged in thirds, i.e., the following: C_6 (C-E-G-A) = Ami_7 and $Ebmi_6$ (Eb-Gb-Bb-C) = $C\emptyset_7$.

SUMMARY: Information for determining chord categories

CHORD TYPES

Major: 1-3-5-7-9-etc.

Minor: 1-b3-5-b7-9-etc.

Dominant: 1-3-5-b7-9-etc.

Diminished: 1-b3-b5-6

Half diminished: 1-b3-b5-b7

Augmented: 1-3-#5

ABBREVIATIONS (using C as root)

C, C $\triangle$, C Major, C Maj_7, C Ma, C Ma_7, C_7, C Maj_7, C M, C M_7

C-, $C-_7$, C min, C min_7, Cmi, Cmi_7, Cm, Cm_7

C_7, C_9, C_{11}, C_{13}

Co, Co_7, C dim, C dim_7

$C\emptyset$, $Cmi_7^{(b5)}$, $C-^{(b5)}$

C+, C_7+, $C_7^{\#5}$, C_7 aug, C_7^{+5}

Alterations and additions are made according to the key of the bottom tone.

CHORD CATEGORIES

I: All major type chords (i.e., C, C_6, all chords with major in the title)

II: All minor type chords (minor in the title) including the $\emptyset_7$

V: Any dominant seventh chord (letter plus a number other than 6); anything other than a major or minor type

Special V chord types: (1) Augmented (Aug=dominant 7th of the same name, i.e., $C+=C_7$)

(2) Diminished. Diminished chords are usually derived from the dominant 7th a major third below the root of the diminished chord, i.e., $Co_7=Ab_7$.

SOME SUGGESTED EXERCISES

1. Name the six chord types and give examples of each.
2. Give an example of an extension to an Ab_7 chord.
3. Build the following chords:

a. Ab 13

b. $G_7^{(+11)}$

c. Dmi_9

d. E

e. $A\emptyset_7$

f. $D_9^{(b11)}$

g. Fo_7

h. $Bbmi_7^{(b5)}$

i. $C_7 \left({}^{\#9}_{\#5} \right)$

j. F#

2

4. Classify the chords in exercise #3 as to major, minor, or dominant function.
5. Give the dominant 7th to which the following diminished chords belong:
    a. Ao_7
    b. Do_7
    c. $F^\#o_7$
    d. Bo_7
    e. Co_7
6. Find the roots of the following chords:
    a. C-E-G-A
    b. B-E-G-A-C
    c. Db-Ab-Bb-F-Gb-Eb
    d. $F^\#$-C-Eb-A
    e. E-B-D-G

C
C C6 CMaj.7 Cmi Cmi6 Cmi7
Db (C#)
Db Db6 DbMaj.7 Dbmi Dbmi6 Dbmi7
D
D D6 DMaj.7 Dmi Dmi6 Dmi7
Eb
Eb Eb6 Eb Maj.7 Eb mi Eb mi6 Eb mi7
E
E E6 E Maj.7 Emi Emi6 Emi7
F
F F6 F Maj.7 Fmi Fmi6 Fmi7
Gb (F#)
Gb Gb6 Gb Maj.7 Gbmi Gbmi6 Gbmi7
G
G G6 G Maj.7 Gmi Gmi6 G mi7
Ab
Ab Ab6 Ab Maj.7 Ab mi Ab mi6 Ab mi7
A
A A6 A Maj.7 Ami Ami6 Ami7
Bb
Bb Bb6 Bb Maj.7 Bbmi Bbmi6 Bbmi7
B
B B6 B Maj.7 Bmi Bmi6 B mi7

Cmi7 (b5) Cmi (maj.7) C7 C aug. (+) C7 (+5) C dim. (o) C7 (b5)
Dbmi7 (b5) Dbmi (maj.7) Db7 Db aug. (+) Db7 (+5) Db dim. (o) Db7 (b5)
Dmi7 (b5) Dmi (maj.7) D7 D aug. (+) D7 (+5) D dim. (o) D7 (b5)
Ebmi7 (b5) Ebmi (maj.7) Eb7 Eb aug. (+) Eb7 (+5) Eb dim. (o) Eb7 (b5)
Emi7 (b5) Emi (maj.7) E7 E aug. (+) E7 (+5) E dim. (o) E7 (b5)
Fmi7 (b5) Fmi (maj.7) F7 F aug. (+) F7 (+5) Fdim. (o) F7 (b5)
Gbmi7 (b5) Gbmi (maj.7) Gb7 Gb aug. (+) Gb7 (+5) Gbdim. (o) Gb7 (b5)
Gmi7 (b5) Gmi (maj.7) G7 G aug. (+) G7 (+5) G dim. (o) G7 (b5)
Abmi7 (b5) Abmi (maj.7) Ab7 Ab aug. (+) Ab7 (+5) Ab dim. (o) Ab7 (b5)
Ami7 (b5) Ami (maj.7) A7 A aug. (+) A7 (+5) A dim. (o) A7 (b5)
Bbmi7 (b5) Bbmi (maj.7) Bb7 Bb aug. (+) Bb7 (+5) Bb dim. (o) Bb7 (b5)
Bmi7 (b5) Bmi (maj.7) B7 B aug. (+) B7 (+5) B dim. (o) B7 (b5)

Chapter II

THE INSTRUMENTS

The instruments of the orchestra are divided into four main sections: brass, woodwinds, strings and percussion.

The Brass section includes such instruments as:

Trumpet	Tenor Trombone
Cornet	Bass Trombone
Bass Trumpet	Baritone Horn
French Horn	Tuba

The Woodwinds include:

Piccolo	Bassoon
Flute	Contra Bassoon
Alto Flute	Soprano Saxophone
Bass Flute	Alto Saxophone
Oboe	Tenor Saxophone
English Horn	Baritone Saxophone
Clarinet	Bass Saxophone
Bass Clarinet	

The Strings include:

Violin	Guitar
Viola	Electric Bass
Violincello	Tenor Banjo
Contrabass	

The Percussion instruments include:

Tympani	Marimba
Snare Drum	Xylophone
Bass Drum	Celesta
Cymbals	Piano
Vibes	Harp

It is beyond the scope of this chapter to go into details about each instrument, its use, characteristics, idiosyncrasies, etc. This chapter will therefore deal with some comparisons between classes of instruments and some general characteristics of each class. A chart indicating ranges and transposition of each instrument follows this chapter.

Comparison of Families of Instruments (1 is the greatest degree; 5 is the weakest degree)

	Strings	Brass	Woodwinds	Saxophones	Percussion
Homogeneity	1	2	4	3	5
Strength	4	2	5	3	1
Uniformity of Register	1	2	4	3	not applicable

CHARACTERISTICS OF THE ORCHESTRAL FAMILIES

BRASS

1. Good blend with other brass instruments.
2. The larger the instrument the more air required.
3. The larger the instrument the less facility and speed (theoretically).
4. All brass instruments built on the overtone series (bugle).
5. Long tones sound louder than short tones except in highly rhythmic passages.
6. High tones on bass instruments sound higher than tones of the same pitch in the low registers of treble instruments.
7. High tones on brass instruments are most prominent.
8. Brass instruments tend toward isolation.
9. Dissonance is particularly acute in brass.
10. Avoid extreme registers.
11. Trumpets and trombones are nearly equal in power; tuba and horn are less strong.
12. Clefs.
    a. Trumpets read in treble clef.
    b. Horns read in treble and bass clef.
    c. Bass trumpet reads in treble clef.
    d. Trombones read in bass, tenor, alto and treble clef. (When in treble clef, transposition is a 9th higher than it sounds.)
    e. Tuba reads in bass clef or tenor clef.

WOODWINDS DIVIDED INTO CLASSES

NON-REEDS	SINGLE REEDS	DOUBLE REEDS
Piccolo	Clarinets	Oboe
Flutes	Bass Clarinets	English Horns
Alto Flute	Saxophones	Bassoon
Bass Flute		Contra Bassoon

Clefs

1. Flutes read in treble clef.
2. Oboes read in treble clef.
3. English Horn reads in treble clef.
4. Clarinets read in treble clef.
5. Bass Clarinet reads in treble and bass clef.
6. Bassoon reads in bass and tenor clef.
7. Contra Bassoon reads in bass clef.
8. Saxophones read in treble clef.

General Characteristics of Woodwinds

1. Woodwinds are the distinctive sound of the four sections.
2. Each solo woodwind has a highly distinctive sound.
3. Each solo woodwind has complete blend potential with all instruments.
4. The tone color of each member of the woodwind family remains constant throughout the range of the instrument but the intensity may vary because of tessitura and technical capacity.

STRINGS

Size Differences

1. Violas are a perfect fifth lower than violins.
2. Cellos are an octave lower than violas.
3. Basses are an octave lower than cellos and sound an octave lower than written.

Clef Differences

1. Violins play in treble clef only.
2. Violas play in alto and treble clef.

3. Cellos play in bass, tenor and treble clef.
4. Basses play in bass, tenor and treble clef. (Always sounding an octave lower than written.)

Unanimities of Strings
1. Open strings are loudest and most prominent. Open strings should usually be avoided in slow or expressive passages.
2. Outside strings are most alive.
3. The larger the instrument the more effective the pizzicatto.
4. The smaller the instrument the more flexibility available and consequently the more activity in the writing.
5. Long chromatic passages should be used judiciously.
6. The trill size determines the facility.
    a. P 4th on violin.
    b. P 4th on viola.
    c. Major 3rd on cello.
    d. Major 2nd on bass.
    e. Minor 3rd on electric bass.
    f. P 4th on guitar.
    g. P 4th on banjo.
7. Short tones played with separate bows sound louder than long tones.

PERCUSSION

1. Two basic types.
    a. Definite pitch—tympani, vibes, xylophone, etc.
    b. Indefinite pitch—drums, cymbals, tom-tom, bongos, etc.

Ranges of Instruments

PERCUSSION

tympani (4)

30"   28'   25"   23"

xylophone   written   sounds an octave higher

marimba   written   sounds an octave higher

vibes

piano   15ma

8va lower

celesta   written   8va   sounds an octave higher

harp   8va

8va lower

11

Chapter III

GENERAL RULES FOR INSTRUMENTAL SCORING

1. Observe the overtone series: wider intervals at the bottom, close intervals at the top. **(example 1)**
2. Write idiomatically. Take into consideration the characteristic tone and individuality of each instrument. **(example 2)**
3. Write in comfortable registers for all instruments.
4. High pitches on all instruments are best led up to.
5. A note tends to sound higher for a lower instrument than the identical note on a higher pitched instrument. **(example 3)**
6. The larger the instrument the less agility.
7. Quick rhythms should be simplified as they approach the lower register. **(example 4)**
8. Remember wind players must **rest.**
9. View all lines as horizontal entities rather than vertical.
10. Always include dynamics, tempo indication and expressive markings.
11. Changes in the type of scoring, grouping of instruments, number of voices, etc., should coincide with the introduction of a new idea, theme or phrase. **(example 5)**
12. Instruments forming chords should be used continuously in the same way during a given passage. (Doubled or not, 4, 5 or 6-way scoring, etc.) **(example 6)** This rule may be violated to insure that a given part is brought out.
13. One of the tasks of a good composer-arranger is to make sure that each part is heard in its proper perspective. To assure prominence in a given part any one of a number of factors may be considered:
    a. Dynamics— added volume in one instrument or reduced volume in the others will produce prominence. **(example 7)**
    b. If all other factors are equal a moving voice will be prominent if the other voices are static. **(example 8)**
    c. Spacing—If **one** instrument is placed at a distance from the other instruments then attention will be drawn to the solitary instrument. **(example 9)**
    d. Rhythm—when the rhythm of one instrument is strikingly different from the other instruments, particularly if it is complex, that instrument will stand out. **(example 10)**
    e. Tessitura—an instrument that remains either in an extreme high register or an extreme low register tends to stand out. **(example 11)**
    f. Physical properties of the instrument. For instance, if a brass instrument is placed in the midst of strings or woodwinds it will be prominent.
    g. How the instruments are combined—if all other things are equal the outer voices will be most prominent. **(example 12)**
14. Except in special cases, an instrument chosen to play a theme should be able to carry it through its entirety. **(example 13)**
15. In a small group it is not often possible to make use of homogeneous groupings. It is, however, possible to create the illusion of a brass section or a saxophone section through the skillful use of the instruments available. For instance, using trumpet, alto, tenor, trombone and bari—countless tonal combinations are possible.

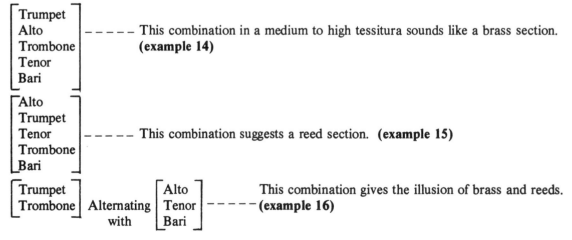

$$\begin{bmatrix} \text{Trumpet (in bucket)} \\ \text{Alto} \\ \text{Tenor} \\ \text{Trombone (in bucket)} \end{bmatrix}$$ – – – – This combination sounds like a French horn section. **(example 17)**

When a brass instrument is in the lead, the group takes on the property of a brass section. When a saxophone leads, then the section assumes the properties of a reed section. The reader is encouraged to experiment with other instrumental combinations.

16. Dissonance tends to be more acute between like instruments, particularly in brass and horns. **(example 18)**

17. Dissonance attenuates when it's between dissimilar instruments and the instruments are placed far apart. **(example 19)**

18. In ordinary small group writing, the instruments are best distributed in their normal order of range. **(example 20)**

General Rules

Chapter IV

CONSTRUCTING A MELODY

All jazz writers and arrangers must learn to compose melodies early in their careers. Jazz arranging consists of much more than orchestration or arranging pretty melodies. All good arrangers must have the equipment to compose their own melodies and to re-compose other melodies.

The tenets of good melody vary with the circumstances, type of tune, style and other considerations. We will first examine some tenets of melody that transcend delimiting styles and definitions. Some of them follow:

1. First, there must be a proper balance of diatonic movement and skips. Stepwise motion is the general rule in melodic construction. To this we add skips for variety.

   Generally, leaps, except along the outline of the chord, turn back in the direction of the skip. However, if the second note of a skip is the final note of a phrase or is followed by a prolonged rest, the melody may continue in the same direction. **(example 1)**

2. A melody should aim in a general manner toward a climax point. All melodies usually have a single climax point or area. This point might be at the highest pitch of an area in which the general tessitura is high. The main thrust of a good melody is to approach and leave this point or series of points in an effective manner. Once a climax is achieved, the melody will usually descend gradually to a point of less intensity. More often than not the lessening of tension and returning to normal is much more rapid than the buildup or ascent. **(example 2)**

3. There must always be contrast and interplay between: density and lack of density, tension and relaxation, and intensity and lack of intensity. **(example 3)**

4. In most melodies there is considerable evidence of repetition which, when combined with other things, acts as a unifying factor; however, the writer is cautioned to avoid too much repetition of a curve, a note or a phrase except for special effect. Repetition in the melody can, however, be sufficiently disguised to allow a more extensive use. The changes which effect the disguise might include alteration of intervals, rhythm, dynamics, etc. **(example 4)**

5. Another general rule to be observed: When the melody is static then the harmony or the rhythm must move. If the melody is active then the other components may be less active. **(example 5)**

6. Most melodies have some unique feature that distinguishes them from other melodies of the same type. The melody might contain a sudden rhythmic shift, a note that sounds wrong, a particular interval that is used more than others or some other such device. **(example 6)**

7. The writer must strive for a proper balance between the new and the old (the novel and the familiar). Every melody must have enough recognizable elements to provide stability but enough of the novel to prevent the listener from anticipating every melodic, harmonic and rhythmic occurence.

8. Melodic phrases are not all the same lengths; length is by and large governed by the idea itself. Long phrases are usually broken into smaller units with implied cadence points. **(example 7)**

9. Avoid outlining chords (tertian, quartal, quintal, etc.) **(example 8)** There are many exceptions to this rule but they are special cases and retain strength and vitality through other means.

   "Freedom Jazz Dance" – Eddie Harris
   " 'Round Midnight" – T. Monk
   "I Can't Get Started" – V. Duke

10. Avoid extreme ranges (generally not larger than an octave and a fifth). **(example 9)**
11. Strive to change melodic direction after four or five tones. Avoid scale units. **(example 10)**
12. Avoid too much repetition of a given tone. **(example 11)** This becomes even more of a problem when the attending note falls the same place in the measure. **(example 11a)**
13. Use augmented and diminished intervals sparingly. **(example 12)**
14. Use chromaticism sparingly (generally not more than three semitones in succession). **(example 13)** Hidden chromaticism is also best avoided. **(example 14)** If more than two tones intervene between a chromatic progression the chromaticism is attenuated. **(example 15)**
15. Limit the melody to two or three basic note values. **(example 16)**

SUGGESTED READING . . .

A Composer's World (chapter 4) by Paul Hindemith

Serial Composition (chapter 5) by Reginald Smith Brindle

Studies in Counterpoint (Introduction; chapters I and II) by Ernst Krênek

The Rhythmic Structure of Music by Cooper and Meyer

Structure and Style (section I) by Leon Stein

The Schillinger System of Musical Composition, Volumes I and II by Joseph Schillinger

Twentieth Century Music Idioms by G. Welton Marquis

Composing for the Jazz Orchestra by William Russo

Composing Music: A New Approach by William Russo with Jeffrey Ainis and David Stevenson

SUGGESTED LISTENING . . .

Listen to any recordings of compositions you enjoy. Pay particular attention to the points raised in this chapter.

SUGGESTED ASSIGNMENTS . . .

1. Study some of your favorite composed melodies with regard to the rules listed in this chapter.
2. Write many fragments.
   a. Not more than two measures in length (six to ten notes).
   b. Simple folk-like melodies.
   c. Avoid finalizing the phrase. Leave it "up in the air." The phrase should want to continue.
   d. Work for a "sing-song" quality.

Constructing A Melody

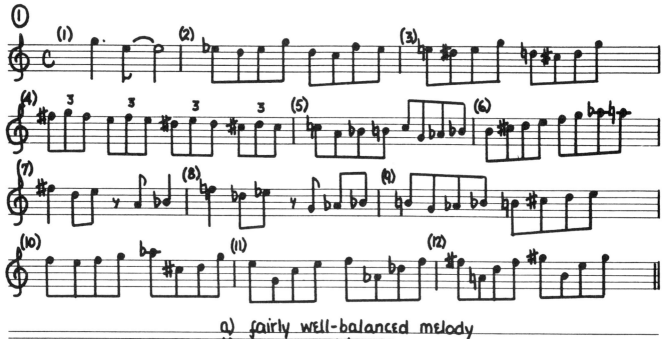

① (1) ... (2) ... (3)
(4) 3 3 3 3 (5) ... (6)
(7) (8) (9)
(10) (11) (12)

a) fairly well-balanced melody
b) Measures 11 & 12 : skips along the chord
c) Measures 7 & 8 return in the direction of the skip

② Refer to number ①. The climax is in measure 6, halfway through, and the descent is about half the tune.

③ 4 choruses

	single time medium range	some double time medium range	double time high range	single time to half time medium to low range
SOLOIST	pp thin texture	mf more involved	ff dense	mf lessening of density

④ Refer to example ①. Measures 2, 3, 5, 11, and 12 are modifications of the same curve.

⑤

Dmi₇ ... ⌐ 3 ⌐ ... Fmi₇ Bb₇ Ebmi₇ Ab₇ ... Etc.

⑥ Refer to example ①. The main unifying factor is the use of alternating half steps and whole steps (diminished scale color) and the implied major triads in measures 1, 7, 8, 10, 11, and 12.

⑦ The first phrase is 4 measures long and dovetails into the second phrase, which is measures 5 & 6. The third phrase is measures 7-12.

⑧ Under normal conditions, avoid circumstances like measures 11 and 12.
This becomes acceptable because of the sequential pattern it forms.

⑨ Range of the example is

⑩ Avoid passages like measures 5 & 6, and 9. These places would be much
more offensive if they were common scales, i.e. major, minor, etc.

⑪ Too much of the note C.

⑪a

⑫

⑬

⑭ OR

⑮ This is satisfactory.

⑯ NOT

Chapter V

TECHNIQUES TO BE USED IN DEVELOPING A MELODY

We will now examine some of the techniques used to develop a melody. Again the over-riding consideration is the use of tension and relaxation.

REPETITION

Repetition is an important unifying principle used in traditional Western music (jazz included). Exact repetition palls very quickly so the task of the writer is to use repetition skillfully and subtly. Exact repetition of an idea more than two times, except for special purposes, is rarely effective. (original theme, **example 1**).

1. One of the easiest techniques for avoiding exact repetition is octave displacement of all or part of a line. Its strength and its weakness is its lack of subtlety. **(example 2)**

2. Another technique for avoiding exact repetition is sequence. Sequence is the technique of transposing a section of a theme by an interval other than an octave. Even sections using this technique become uncomfortable to listen to after two or three repetitions. **(example 3)**

     The technique is considerably more effective if slight changes are made in the sequences, i.e.:
   a. Changes of contour
   b. Harmonic changes $\Big\}$ **(example 4)**
   c. Rhythmic changes
   d. Altered notes

3. Extension is a technique of modification in which a phrase is extended to include more measures than its original form. The process might take place over many measures with a note or notes being added to each subsequent repetition. This technique is particularly effective in a situation where the harmony is slow-moving or static (i.e., *"So What," "Speak Low,"* the blues, etc.) **(example 5)**

4. Truncation is the technique of omitting a note or notes from the end of a musical phrase. As with extension, the process may take place over an extended period of time, and, as with extension, the technique is particularly effective in a situation where the harmony is slow-moving or static.

     Both truncation and extension are more effective when the phrases which utilize the technique are consecutive; however, the technique is still useful as long as the phrases are close enough together to be remembered and perceived as modifications of the same basic idea. **(example 6)**

     Thelonious Monk's *"Straight No Chaser"* is a marvelous written example of both extension and truncation.

5. Augmentation or elongation refers to the process of increasing the rhythmic values of a theme. This is usually done by increasing the value of the notes by a constant ratio. **(example 7)** (A caution: Don't stretch the theme too much, as this causes it to lose its identity.)

6. Diminution is the process of decreasing the rhythmic values of a theme. This is usually done by decreasing the value of the notes by a constant ratio. **(example 8)**

     In an actual jazz situation, augmentation and diminution are rarely used in a pure form and are generally used briefly, modified and in combination with each other and other developmental techniques.

7. Fragmentation is the technique of presenting the theme in parts. This particular technique is very popular with many jazz writers (Monk, J. J. Johnson, John Lewis, etc.). Almost all jazz composers use this technique consciously or otherwise. **(example 9)**

8. All motifs or themes have four basic forms: original, inversion, retrograde and retrograde inversion.
   a. Inversion changes each ascending interval into the corresponding descending interval and vice versa. **(example 10)**
   b. Retrograde is the playing of a theme backwards (beginning with the last note and ending with the first one). **(example 11)**
   c. Retrograde inversion is the technique of combining retrograde and inversion or playing a line upside down and backwards. **(example 12)**

     Inversion, retrograde and retrograde inversion are not generally considered practical or musically feasible for use in the jazz context except in extremely modified form. These strictly calculated practices are the antithesis of jazz. Usually a musical hint of one or more of the three techniques is enough to convey the basic idea.

9. Rhythmic and melodic displacement is the technique of removing a theme or rhythm from its usual position in the time or harmony. **(example 13)**

10. Contextual placement for consonance or dissonance is a technique of placing a theme or section of a theme within the harmony in such a manner as to render the theme consonant or dissonant by context. In most cases the theme remains unaltered. **(example 14)**

11. Tonal shift refers to the technique of arbitrarily moving a theme or theme fragment to another key area, irrespective of the underlying harmony. This is a technique practiced more and more by modern writers to add harmonic and melodic interest to the line. **(example 15)**

12. Change of mode is simply the technique of changing the scale color of the theme or theme fragment, i.e., from major scale color to harmonic minor ascending color. **(example 16)**

13. Juxtaposition of tune sections is the process of using the material from one section in another section (verbatim or altered). **(example 17)**

14. Simplifying or complicating the line. Simplification takes place when we **remove** everything but the essence of the line (getting rid of embellishing and decorating material). **(example 18)** Complication takes place when we **add** embellishing and decorative or additional material to the line. **(example 19)**

15. Alteration of shape. **(example 20)**
   a. Changing the size of the interval.
   b. Changing the contour of the line.

16. Combining elements of the composition at random simply means joining measures together that were formerly segregated. **(example 21)**

17. Isolating and using rhythmic aspects of composition, i.e., using unique rhythmic factors. **(example 22)**

A number of complete original compositions with analysis follow:

LE ROI

1. The same phrase is used three times (centers around C).
2. 3/4 material is the same as the beginning material.
3. Recurring curves.

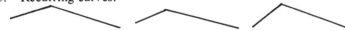

4. Range is a ninth.
5. All phrases are four measures long.
6. Two basic scales or modes.

THREE VIGNETTES

1. Form is unique in that it contains three complete compositions in one.
2. All three compositions are extremely long-lined and lyrical.

Composition I

1. Form A A B A
      8 8 8 9
2. Germ motive in (A) 1 - 2 is used in 3 - 4 and 5 - 6 in slightly altered form. (B) same germ but moved over one measure.
3. Narrow range.

Composition II

1. A   B   A
   7   9   7
2. Composed line measure three gives the feeling of being an improvised accompaniment.
3. Unusually large skips.
4. Few basic rhythms.
5. Sequences 3 and 5 again, 6 and 9 (same two-note figure in diminution and augmentation).

Melody III

1. Form 3 A ‖ A 4   13 ‖ 3   (A)
         4 ‖   4   ‖ 4
         26 ‖ 25 ├── 10 ──┤ ├── 25 ──┤
2. Range—an octave and a fourth.
3. Melody line again includes its own accompaniment.

4.   Predominance of skips of a fourth and a fifth.
5.   Phrases overlap in the (A) section.
6.   Two or three basic figures.
7.   (B) 1, 3, 8, 9 same rhythmic figure and curve.
8.   Although the return of (A) is the same length as the first (A), an extension is built in.

JUST BEFORE SEPTEMBER

1.   Form A A B A
2.   Melody moves freely through many keys.
3.   Balance between diatonic movement and skips.
4.   Melodies often outline chords.
5.   Two or three basic rhythms.
6.   Melodies are most often of a lush melodic variety (C Major 7, 9, 11, etc.)
7.   Range—an octave and a fourth.
8.   Curves vary considerably.
9.   (A) 5 - 8 phrases dovetail.
10. (B) material contrasts (A) material but the illusion is that the composition is through composed.

APRIL B

1.   Unusual form

2.   Pickups to (A) same as pickups to (B).
3.   The Bass figure in (C) starts as accompaniment and then becomes the melody.
4.   Measure (A) 5 is return of skip.
5.   (A) climaxes in measure 5.
6.   Same melody but altered in (B) 2, 4, 8, 10, 12.
7.   Two measure phrases.

THE LITTLE PRINCESS

1.   Form A A B A
            16 16 16 16
2.   (A) section—two notes ascending then two notes descending—two notes ascending with extension (1–4). (A) 5 - 8 more extension. (A) slightly altered.
3.   Scales - sequence twice - then slightly
     1 - 2   3 - - 8
     altered cadence.
     Three sets of sequences taken from (A) 3 through 8.
4.   Diminution of rhythmic figures and harmonic, rhythmic and melodic sequences.
5.   Relatively narrow range (octave and a second with one high point).

SOFT SUMMER RAIN

1.   Regular A A B A form.
            8   8 8 8
2.   Unique features—opening figure c a g permeates the entire tune.

     (A) 1, 4, 5, 6, 7, 8

     (B) 2, 3, 6 in sequence, inversion and altered intervals.

     Measure (A) 7 is altered augmentation of (A) 2, (A) 3 is an inversion.
3.   (B) 5 - 6 have identical chord sequences but different melodies (slightly altered).
4.   Two or three basic rhythms.

THE I.U. SWING MACHINE

1.   Unique factors—uneven sections

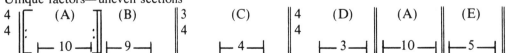

2. Combination of major and minor tonality.
3. Range two octaves and a fourth (unusual).
4. The recurrent anticipated fourth beat.
5. The entire tune is built on the germ found in measure two.
   It is found in Measure (A) 3 - 4 - 8
                         (B) 1 - 2 - 3 - 9
              Tag (E)   3
   germ with extension (A) 5 - 9
                       (B) 3 - 9
            sequence (C)
                    (D)

6. (B) E^bmi B^bmi | E^bmi B^bmi | E^bmi | B^bmi   Augmentation
          //   //   //   //

7. G^b | F | G^b | This three grouping prepares the (C) 3/4 section.
   //// | //// | //// |

8. The measure of (B) is also the (E) melody.
9. (A) 1 through 10 is really one phrase broken into sections.
10. (A) 8 is an inversion of (A) 7.
11. (A) 3 - 4 same changes as (B) 1 - 2 - 3 - 4.
12. Whole step movement
    (A) 1 - 2
    (B) 7 - 8 - 9
13. Tonal shift occurs in the 3/4 section.
14. Juxtaposition of tune sections. Material in (A) 10 same as bridge.

J IS FOR LOVELINESS

1. Regular A A B A form.
      8 8 8 8
2. Unique features—whole step movement of chords:
                   (A) 4 - 6, (A) 7 - 8
                   (B) 3, 5 - 6 - 7
   Chords are frequently outlined pickups, (A) 7, (B) 6.
3. Sequences
   (A) 1 - 2 - 3 - 5, (B) 7 - 8, (B) 2 - 3, 4 - 5
   (B) 5 and 6 with rhythmic displacement.
4. Odd harmonizations.
5. Climax in measure (B) 4.
6. Variation of pickup and pickup to (A) 2. (Just a subtle change.)
7. Three basic rhythms.

BLACK THURSDAY

1. Regular A A B A form.
      8 8 8 8
2. Unique features—medium range but a narrow tessitura.
                  (12th)   (6th)
3. Two or three basic rhythms.
4. Melodic germ in measures (A) 1 - 2 is inverted in (A) 7 - 8 and (B) 5 - 6.
5. Exact repetition in measure (A) 1 - 4.
6. (B) 1 - 2 is a form of (A) 5 - 6.
7. Unusual instances in which changes and melody both move rapidly.

PASSION

1. Regular A A B A form.
      8 8 8 8
2. Unique features—melody is in one key essentially with some movement away from the key center. Three repeated notes in (A) 2 and (B) 2 and 7.

3. Chords move when the melody stands still.

                   1st   ‖   2nd

(A) 3 - 4   7 - 8   ‖ 7 - 8

Chords static when melody moves (B) 1 - 2.

4. The first eight climaxes in measure five—the bridge climaxes in measure one.

5. Sequences

    (A) 1 - 4 with alteration.

    (B) 5 - 6

6. The chord changes outline a diminished scale.

KENTUCKY OYSTERS

1. Form   3/4   24 measures blues

2. Measure Sequences   Sequences

    1 - 2   3 - 4

    5 - 6 (with alterations)   7 - 8 (Inversion of 3 - 4)

    9 - 10   11 - 12 (slightly altered)

    Measure 21 is a combination of both sequences.

    Measures 17 - 18 - 19 - 20 with arpeggios.

3. Long held notes add interest.

4. Two or three basic note values.

THE PROFESSOR

1. Form

    A   B   C   3   D   pickups   A

  ⊢— 18 —⊣ ‖ ⊢— 9 —⊣ ‖ ⊢— 6 —⊣ | 4 ⊢— 8 —⊣ ‖   ⊢—10—⊣ ‖

2. (A)   Sequence   Extensions

    1 ——————————— 2 + 3   4 ——————— 10

    (B) Contrasting material

    1 - 4 measure phrase 5 - 9

    Shifting rhythmic feel extension of first 4.

    (C) Triad + scale

    (D) Scale melody built from diminished scale.

TERRIBLE "T"

1. Form—Blues (24 measures)
2. Melody is extremely angular.
3. Balance between movement and staticness.
4. Balance between skips and diatonic movement.
5. Use of diminished scale in measures 17 and 18.
6. Written out slurs which sound improvised. (measures 11 - 12)
7. Notice sustained tones at ends of sections which contain great activity.
8. Recurring sequence—measure before the double bar and measures 7 - 8 - 24.
9. Range—one octave and a minor sixth.
10. Sequential triplet across the bar line in measures 19 - 20 and 21 - 22.

THEME

1. Form is A A B

         8 8 10

                                               A with extension

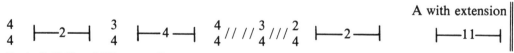

2. Prokofieff-like shifting tonality.
3. Balance between skipwise and stepwise movements.
4. Perfect 4th interval is prominent.
5. Dodecaphonic.
6. Meter follows the flow of line.
7. Extension measures 3 and 4 from the end are an inversion of 1 and 2.

8. Last measure is the same as the opening measure.
9. Each cadence, excluding the final one, leaves the melody dangling.
10. Sequences

    $\frac{3}{4}$ measures 1 and 2.

    Last (A) measures 5 and 6.

    Last 3 measures.

HORN SONATA

1. Throughcomposed.
2. 15 measures long.
3. Octave and a 5th.
4. Balance between skips and diatonic movement.
5. Sequences 1 - 2 - 3

                    10 - 11 and 15

                    12 - 13
6. Extension in measures 10 thru 15.

    Version II is an improvement because of the less obvious sequences in measures 2 and 3.

SUGGESTED READING . . .

Serial Composition (chapters 14 and 15) by Reginald Smith Brindle

Techniques of Twentieth Century Composition (chapters 12 and 13) by Leon Dallin

Jazz: An Introduction to Its Musical Basis (chapter 2) by Avril Dankworth

The Schillinger System of Musical Composition, Volumes I and II by Joseph Schillinger

Twentieth Century Music Idioms by G. Welton Marquis

Composing for the Jazz Orchestra by William Russo

Composing Music: A New Approach by William Russo with Jeffrey Ainis and David Stevenson

SUGGESTED LISTENING . . .

Play records of your favorite composers. Identify the various techniques described in this chapter.

SUGGESTED ASSIGNMENTS . . .

1. Locate and write down in a notebook for future reference examples from recordings of each of the techniques described in this chapter.
2. Write a 32-measure melody according to the following specifications:
    a. A A B A form.
    b. One high and one low point in both the (A) and the (B) sections.
    c. Not to exceed an octave and a fourth in range.
    d. No more than three different note values.
    e. (A) section essentially diatonic.
        (B) section essentially angular.
    f. Use repetition, but never use an exact repeat more than twice. (Use variation technique.)
    g. Use at least one example of extension and two examples of sequence.
    h. Have at least one identifying or unique factor. (Rhythmic or melodic and should occur more than once.)
    i. Ballad tempo.
3. Write other melodies according to your own specifications.

Developing A Melody

26

(1st 3 measures inverted)

27

⑪ Refer to the material in example 🄰. This is the first four measures backwards.

⑫ Refer to example 🄰. This is the retrograde inversion.

⑬ Refer to example 🄰

⑭ Refer to example 🄰

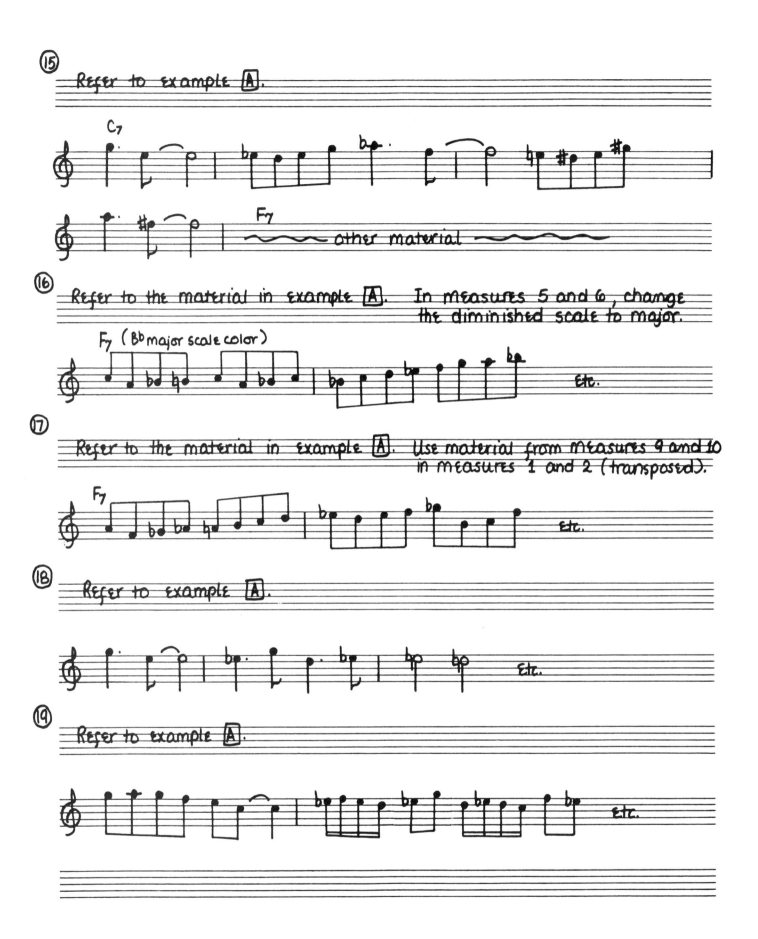

⑮ Refer to example Ⓐ.

⑯ Refer to the material in example Ⓐ. In measures 5 and 6, change the diminished scale to major.

⑰ Refer to the material in example Ⓐ. Use material from measures 9 and 10 in measures 1 and 2 (transposed).

⑱ Refer to example Ⓐ.

⑲ Refer to example Ⓐ.

LeRoi

Recorded versions may be found on the following albums:

ESP 1059   Eastern Man Alone

                               Charles Tyler

Atlantic 1428   Together

                      Philly Joe Jones and Elvin Jones

Fermata FB-97   Impacto

                       Hector Costita Serteto

Three Vignettes

Tune III

Just Before September

April B

The Little Princess

36

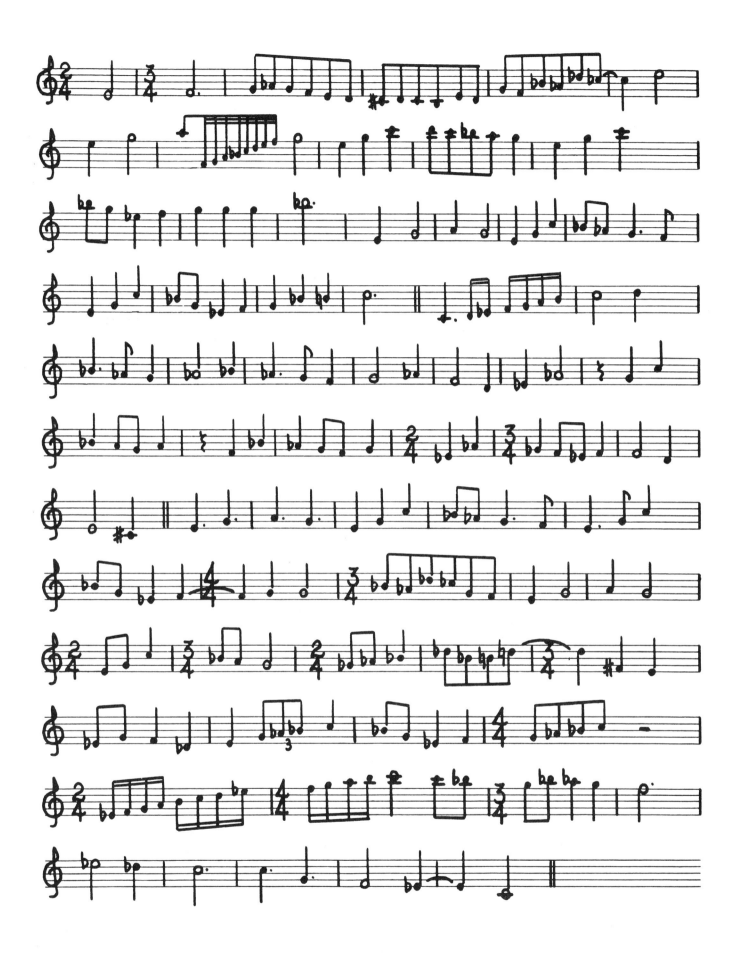

The I. U. Swing Machine

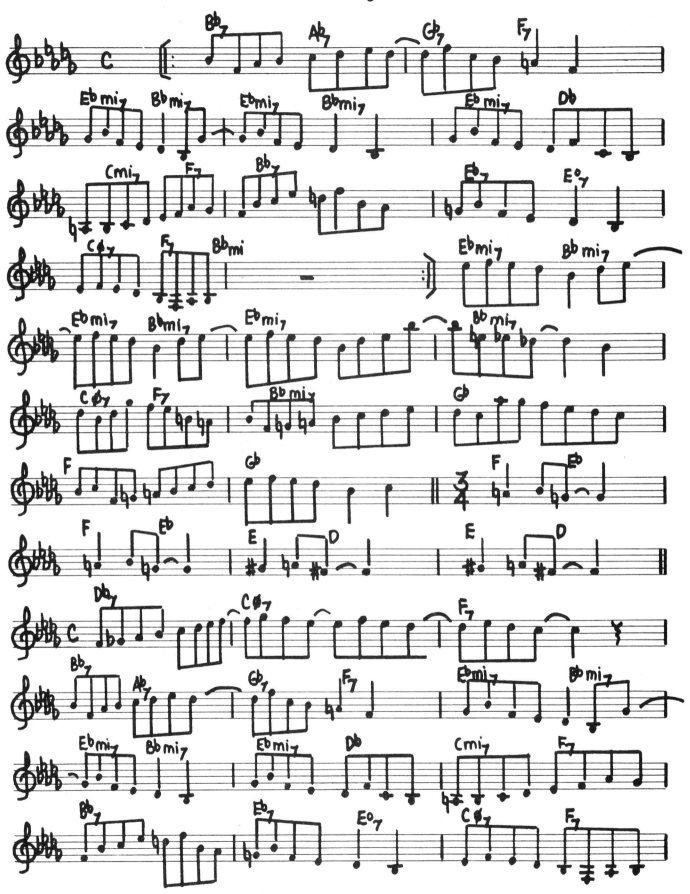

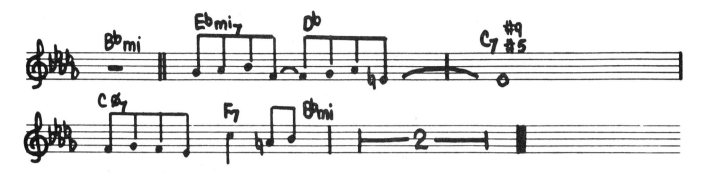

Recorded version may be found on :
Silver Crest CBD-69-6A   C.B.D. N.A.

Soft Summer Rain

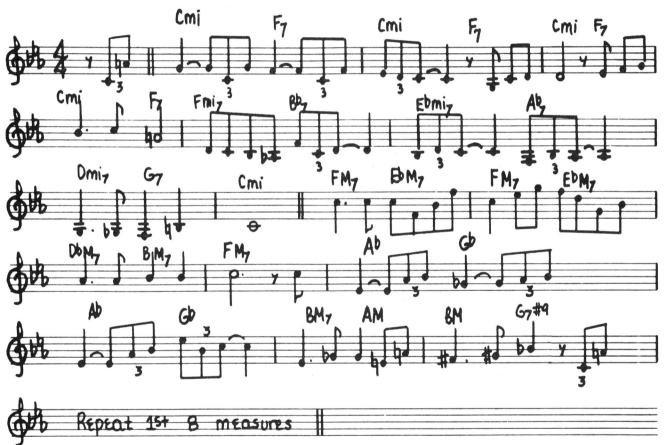

Repeat 1st 8 measures

Recorded versions may be found on the following albums:
CBD-69-68   C. B. D. N. A   (Silver Crest Records)
Blue Note BST-84328 Song For My Daughter
Jack Wilson

J Is For Loveliness

Recorded version may be found on:

Isis I-608

Black Thursday

Terrible T

Passion

Kentucky Oysters

Recorded version may be found on:
Riverside RLP341   Stratusphunk

George Russell Sextet

42

The Professor

Chapter VI

FITTING CHORDS TO A GIVEN MELODIC LINE

One of the most difficult tasks facing the jazz arranger-composer is that of ascertaining the harmonization to a given melody line. The arranger-composer might encounter the problem when:

1. He attempts to harmonize an original melody of his own.
2. He attempts to harmonize someone else's melody, i.e., standard, jazz tune, etc.
3. He attempts to check the harmonization in a "fake" book (often wrong) or on a piece of sheet music (often pedestrian).

This chapter will concern itself with some general and specific rules for dealing with these situations.

1. Make sure that you know the melody, that you are able to sing or play it correctly. Very often we have only a vague impression of a melody culled from a record or some other source. It is **absolutely necessary** to be able to reproduce the melody correctly before proceeding to the next steps.
2. Try to ascertain the key.
   a. Check key signature if possible.
   b. Play or sing the melody, stopping at phrase ends to check resolving tendencies. From each of these points of rest try to sing or play to the tonic of the key. **(example 1)**
3. Reduce the melody to its essentials; simplify the melodic line, getting rid of embellishing tones, appoggiatura and other decorative material. **(example 2)**
4. Find a bass line that sounds good against the melody **then** fill in the chords.
5. Check to see if the tune is subsumed under another structural and/or harmonic type. (Blues, I Got Rhythm, etc.) Many bebop tunes are based on the changes to standard tunes.
6. Generally, the slower the tempo the faster the harmonic rhythm and conversely the faster the tempo the slower the harmonic rhythm. **(example 3)**
7. Check the possibilities for the use of harmonic formulae. Do sections of the tune lend themselves to certain established formulae such as: II V_7 or I VI II V_7 etc.? **(example 4)** Check those sections of the tune where turnarounds of certain types would normally be found. (Last two measures of sections, etc.) **(example 5)**
8. Work backwards from ends of phrases or points of rest, places where the chord is known or at least suspected. For instance, if the last chord is a tonic chord, check to see if it is preceded by a II V_7 progression or one of its substitutions. **(example 6)**
   a. Check for V_7's or II V_7's leading to each new key area. **(example 7)**
   b. Look for logical root movement (refer to the chart of root progressions on page 51).
9. Look for cadence and semi-cadence points with their traditionally-implied chords.
10. Look for resolving tendencies of the melody notes, for instance $^b7$'s down a half step to the 3rd of another chord. **(example 8)**
11. Test seemingly logical formulae against melody notes for discrepancies or verification. **(example 9)**
12. Look for obvious formulae but don't close your mind to other possibilities.
13. Within the bar, assign as many notes as possible to the same chord, particularly at fast tempos. **(example 10)**
    a. Look for chord outlines (explicit or implicit); (obvious or disguised). **(example 11)**
    b. Look for scales, scale fragments that suggest certain chords or tonal areas. **(example 12)**
14. Harmonic changes usually follow the bar line or the normal division of the bar. For example, in a 4/4 measure the harmonic changes would occur on the first or the third beat as opposed to the second and fourth or a fraction of the beat. **(example 13)** Avoid carrying a change across the bar line.
15. With the exception of the dominant 7th chord, avoid having strings of chords of the same quality in succession, i.e., major 7th, minor 7th, etc. **(example 14)** The problem is not so acute in chromatic situations. **(example 15)**
16. Try to recall similar melodies and how they are harmonized.
17. Set up **sure** harmonies and fill in all the "jigsaw" puzzle. **(example 16)**
18. Avoid the Bach chorale approach except for substitution or variation. The Bach chorale approach is simply a chord change for each note. Obviously this kind of harmonization will pose great problems in compositions that will serve as improvisational vehicles. **(example 17)**

19. Try to ascertain the style, period, composer, type of tune, etc. All of these things can provide valuable insights into harmonization of the tune. For instance, a bebop tune would receive a completely different harmonization from a modal tune or a Dixieland tune. **(example 18)**

20. If the tune is familiar it may be possible to remember and recreate the changes you first heard associated with it.

21. Check for **melodic sequences** which might in turn dictate harmonic sequences. **(example 19)**

22. Once you've arrived at a set of harmonic changes that sound correct, then look for similar construction at other places in the composition. **(example 20)**

23. Work for something that sounds correct.

24. The ear is the arbiter.

Fitting Chords to a Given Melodic Line

47

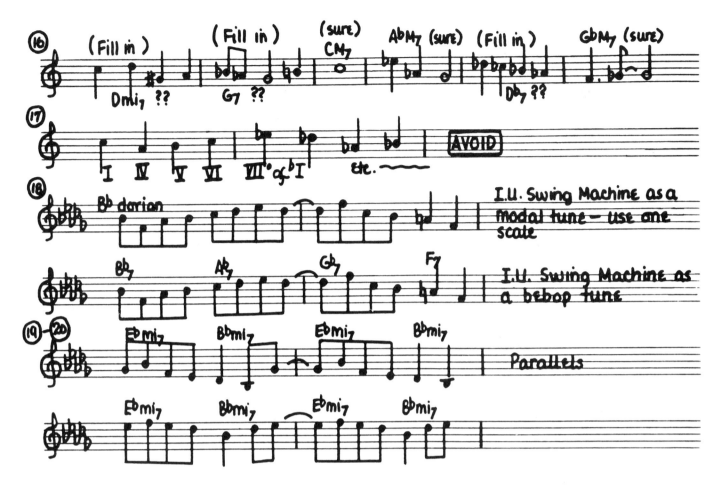

Fitting Chords to a Melody:
Melodies To Be Harmonized

Chart of Logical Root Movements
(Chart moves from strong to weak, from top to bottom)

Chapter VII

WRITING FOR THE RHYTHM SECTION

The term rhythm section in jazz refers to the instruments in a jazz group normally entrusted with the time continuum. This rhythm section can include piano, organ, bass, guitar, drums, vibes and/or miscellaneous percussion. For our purposes we will limit this chapter to piano, guitar, bass and drums.

THE PIANO

The role of the piano in the modern rhythm section is to provide harmonic ostinato, rhythmic impetus, contrapuntal interplay with the soloist and to provide introductions, interludes and endings as well as solos.

In order to provide the pianist with a wide degree of latitude, most modern writers observe a few rules of thumb.

1. Chord symbols including alterations are normally used instead of written out parts except in special situations. **(example 1)** Some situations that might necessitate writing out a complete part might be:
   a. When a particular voicing is needed. **(example 2)**
   b. When a written solo is necessary. **(example 3)**
2. It is often necessary to write a lead line because of certain rhythms you want played or certain melodies played and/or doubled. **(example 4)** (Rhythms are also indicated by notes with (X) heads.) **(example 5)**
3. The use of vergules and chord symbols allows the pianist to exercise his imagination and generally superior knowledge of his instrument (unless, of course, the writer is also a pianist).
4. Special instructions regarding styles, musical mannerisms, etc., may be indicated in writing or a few measures may be written out to indicate the effect desired. **(example 6)** Caution—remember to cancel special effects by writing "swing," "straight ahead," etc.
5. Behind a vocalist, in order to provide a more sensitive accompaniment, it is often good to provide the melody line. This enables a pianist to avoid melodic clashes in his accompaniment and to provide intelligent "fills." **(example 7)**
6. Certain standard short cuts may be used in writing a piano part. **(example 8)**
7. It is often better to omit the piano in tutti sections.

The writer should listen to as many pianists as possible in an effort to find a way to write idiomatically for the piano.

SUGGESTED READING . . . PIANO

Jazz Improvisation (chapter XVI) by David Baker
Jerry Coker's Jazz Keyboard by Jerry Coker
Jazz/Rock Voicings for the Contemporary Keyboard Player by Dan Haerle

THE GUITAR

The rules for writing for guitar are the same as those for piano.

THE BASS

In most pre-avant garde groups, the prime function of the bass player has been to provide a harmonic and rhythmic ostinato in conjunction with the piano. The bass player has been traditionally assigned the task of "walking a line" built on the chords of the tune. The mechanics of constructing a bass line are best left to the bass player (unless the writer happens to be a bass player). Some general guidelines for writing a bass part follow:

1. Chord symbols are normally used instead of written-out parts except in special situations. **(example 1)** Introductions, interludes, endings, unisons, vamps and orchestral tutti are special situations frequent in stylized music such as rhythm & blues music, Latin music and other types that use extensive ostinati. **(example 2)**
2. The use of chord symbols with vergules is often combined with written notes to indicate special rhythms or special parts. **(example 3)**
3. Special instructions regarding style, musical mannerisms, etc., may be indicated in writing or a few measures may be written out to indicate the effect desired. **(example 4)**

If it becomes necessary to write out bass lines the author suggests a thorough study of chapter XVII in *Jazz Improvisation* by the author.

The aspiring writer should listen to bass players in an effort to find a way to write idiomatically for bass.

SUGGESTED READING . . . BASS

The Monk Montgomery Electric Bass Method by Monk Montgomery. Edited and compiled by David Baker.

Jazz Improvisation (chapter XVII) by David Baker

The Evolving Bassist by Rufus Reid

Modern Walking Bass Technique by Mike Richmond

Big Band Bass by John Clayton, Jr.

Electric Bass by Carol Kaye

THE DRUMS

The drummer functions in different ways in different groups. Some of the things that determine how he is to function are: style of group, size of group, abilities of the group, era which it represents, and many other musical and non-musical factors.

Traditionally there seem to be certain functions assigned to a drummer and these functions vary only in degree. The first function is to provide a rhythmic time continuum. This is usually done by assigning certain uses to certain parts of the drum set. The four main parts are: (1) Hi-hat cymbal, (2) Ride cymbal, (3) Bass drum and (4) Snare drum.

The hi-hat (sock) cymbal usually plays on beats two and four in 4/4 time, on beats two and three or on beat two in 3/4 time, etc. **(example 1)**

In order to provide the drummer with maximum latitude, most modern writers observe the following rules:

1. Indicate the form of the tune in the following manner. **(example 2)**
2. Indicate special beats, changes of moods, changes of color, etc., in writing or by writing a few measures to indicate the desired effect. **(example 3)**
3. Indicate special rhythmic effects in one of the following ways. **(example 4)**
4. In places where "fills" or accents are desired, write the rhythm of the melody line or a fragment of the line allowing the drummer to use his expertise. **(example 5)**
5. In stylized music it might be necessary to write a few measures of the "beat" or "rhythm" you desire. (i.e., rhythm & blues, certain Latin beats, calypso, ostinati, etc.) **(example 6)**
6. Always indicate anything unusual or out of the ordinary.

The aspiring writer should listen to as many drummers in an ensemble situation as possible to determine how to write idiomatically for drums.

SUGGESTED READING . . . DRUMS

Jazz Improvisation (chapter XVIII) by David Baker

Complete Instruction in Jazz Ensemble Drumming by Jake Jerger

Latin-American Rhythm Instruments and How To Play Them by Humberto Morales in collaboration with Henry Adler

Drumming the Latin-American Way by Isabelo Ernesto Marrero

SUGGESTED LISTENING . . .

Any Miles Davis recording featuring the rhythm section of Red Garland, Paul Chambers, and Philly Joe Jones; Red Garland, Paul Chambers, and Jimmy Cobb; Wynton Kelly/Bill Evans, Paul Chambers, and Philly Joe Jones/Jimmy Cobb; or Herbie Hancock, Ron Carter, and Tony Williams.

The John Coltrane Quartet rhythm sections.

The rhythm sections of various editions of the Horace Silver Quintets, Art Blakey and the Jazz Messengers, and the Modern Jazz Quartet.

SUGGESTED ASSIGNMENTS . . .

1. Study the scores in the back of this book for insights into how to use the rhythm section.
2. Write rhythm section parts to some of your favorite arrangements on records.

Writing For The Rhythm Section

(similé or continue in the same style)

DRUMS

Chapter VIII

THE PIANO TRIO

The rhythm section of the jazz band often functions as an independent jazz unit if the section is piano, bass and drums. This aggregation is often referred to as a piano trio.

Writing for this group poses some very special problems. Some rules and general procedural techniques follow:

1. A lot more attention must be given to introduction, interludes, modulations and endings. The absence of a horn player means that the writer must rely less on texture for contrast.
2. Introductions, etc., are very effective if there is much rhythmic activity with all three instruments duplicating the rhythm patterns. **(example 1)**
3. Usually, unexpected chord movement and high incidence of chord substitution is extremely effective. **(example 2)**
4. Usually the trio demands much more actual written material than would be expected under other circumstances. The score might be entirely written out in some sections and in other sections abbreviations might be used. **(example 3)**
5. Extremely rhythmic block chords might be used in the matter of a brass section as "send off" into choruses. **(example 4)** Piano might imitate various sections of the jazz band. **(example 5)**
6. Other means of obtaining contrast might include modulations (between soloists or between piano solos); interludes to introduce different sections of the solo; rubato vs. tempoed sections; changes of meter, tempo, mood, dynamic, etc. **(example 6)**
7. Generally there is much more of a propensity for uniformity of rhythmic patterns than in other type groups. **(example 7)**
8. Generally all three instruments are expected to solo. **(example 8)**
9. Rhythmic ostinati and vamps assume much importance in writing for this combination. **(example 9)**
10. All the colors of the various instruments should be exploited, (i.e., pizzicato bass, muted bass, arco, piano in the strings, various mallets, different drums, etc.) **(example 10)**
11. Remember all instruments needn't play all the time.
12. Medleys, extended compositions, etc., are very effective for this combination.

SUGGESTED LISTENING . . .

Any recording of the Ahmad Jamal Trio

Any recording of the Oscar Peterson Trio

Any recording of the Bill Evans Trio

Any recording of the Nat King Cole Trio

McCoy Tyner: *Super Trios* (Milestone M-55003)

McCoy Tyner: *Nights of Ballads and Blues* (Impulse Stereo A-39)

Chick Corea: *Now He Sings, Now He Sobs* (Solid State SS 18039)

Red Garland: *Crossings* (Galaxy GXY-5106)

SUGGESTED ASSIGNMENTS . . .

1. Listen to some of the suggested records and make sketches of the various formats used.
2. Write several **rhythmic** introductions, interludes and endings for a piano trio.
3. Write several arrangements in which the piano imitates sections of a big band.
4. Write an arrangement using a format of your own choosing.

Piano Trio

② original
Dmi₇   G₇   C   C

subsitute
Dmi₇   E♭₇   A♭M₇   B₇   EM₇   G₇   CM₇

substitute
Dmi₇   G₇   A♭mi₇   D♭₇   CM₇   F₇ (+11)   CM₇

SEE substitution chart

57

Chapter IX

THE JAZZ QUARTET

The jazz quartet in this chapter refers to a piano trio plus a solo instrument (horn, guitar, vibes, etc.). All of the rules listed for the piano trio are still in effect when writing for the jazz quartet.

Some other rules follow:

1. Make extensive use of the imitation of big band writing (using the soloist as lead and the piano as a section underneath). **(example 1)**
2. Contrast soloist and rhythm section.
3. Use the soloist in duet with the various rhythm section instruments. (i.e., alto sax and bass or alto sax and drums, etc.) Observe the rules for two-voice writing.
4. Unison writing, tutti or soloist, with another instrument (rhythm) is very effective if used judiciously. **(example 2)**

SUGGESTED LISTENING . . .

Any recording of the Modern Jazz Quartet

Any recording of the John Coltrane Quartet

Any J. J. Johnson Quartet recording

SUGGESTED ASSIGNMENTS . . .

1. Listen to some of the suggested recordings and make sketches of the various formats used.
2. Write several arrangements utilizing the concepts described in this chapter and in the chapter on the piano trio.

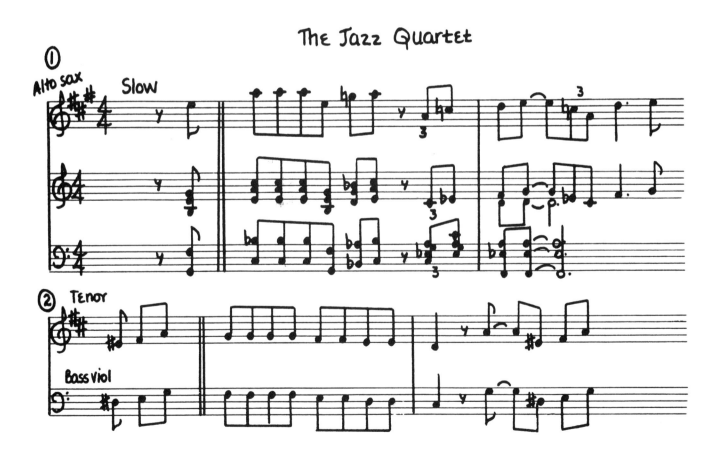

The Jazz Quartet

Chapter X

SCALES AND THEIR RELATIONSHIP TO CHORDS

The following scales and their modes are the most used scales in jazz: major, ascending melodic minor, whole tone, diminished, blues, pentatonic, and, most importantly, the bebop scales.

THE MAJOR SCALE AND ITS DERIVATIVES

C major 7, 9, 11, 13 (major)

D minor 7, 9, 11, 13 (dorian)

G_7 9, 11, 13 (mixolydian)

Bø   (locrian)

THE SCALE ABOVE CONTAINS THE FOLLOWING:

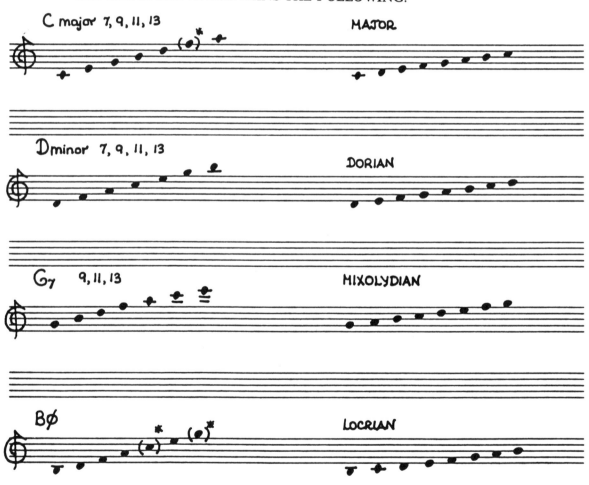

* (   ) the parentheses indicate notes which are usually altered.

In the key of C the chords used in improvisation are C (I), Dmi$_7$ (II), G$_7$ (V), and Bϕ (VII). The rules are as follows:

1. Major chords (I) use the major scale of the same name, i.e., C $\triangle$ = C major scale
2. Minor chords (II) use the major scale a whole step below or the dorian scale of the same name, i.e., Dmi$_7$ = C major scale or D dorian scale
3. Dominant chords (V) use the major scale a fourth above or the mixolydian of the same name, i.e., G$_7$ = C major scale or G mixolydian scale
4. Half diminished chords (VII) (ϕ, mi$_7^{(b5)}$) use the major scale one half step above or the locrian scale of the same name, i.e., Bϕ = C major scale or B locrian scale

Because of the many inconsistencies that exist between theory and performance the major scale is one of the most difficult scales to use and almost always comes replete with admonitions with regard to avoid tones. For example, don't emphasize the perfect fourth of the major scale over a major chord (if the chord is a final chord use a #4 in the scale); over a half diminished chord avoid the tonic of the major scale. The consequence of these traditions and conventions is a complete set of understood approaches to the major scale, including added chromatic tones and other mechanisms that aid in the circumvention of many of these problems; these solutions are dealt with in the section on the bebop scales.

THE ASCENDING MELODIC MINOR SCALE

The ascending melodic minor scale contains five modes which are among the most important in jazz. The scales/modes and the chords to which they relate are as follows:

1. Minor chords with a major 7th use the ascending melodic minor scale of the same name as the chord in question, i.e., Cmi $\triangle$ = the C ascending melodic minor scale
2. Dominant seventh chords with a raised 11th use the ascending melodic minor scale a perfect fifth above the name of the chord in question, i.e., F$_{13}^{(#11)}$ = the C ascending melodic minor scale
3. Dominant seventh chords with a raised 9th or a combination of raised 9th and raised 5th use the ascending melodic minor scale a half step above the name of the chord in question, i.e., B$_7^{(#9)}$ or B$_7$ ($^{#9}_{#5}$) = the C ascending melodic minor scale

4. Half diminished chords with a major 9th use the ascending melodic minor scale a minor third above the name of the chord in question, i.e., Aϕ(Major 9) = the C ascending melodic minor scale
5. Major chords with a raised 5th and a raised 4th use the ascending melodic minor scale a major sixth above the name of the chord in question, i.e., Eb $\triangle$ $^{#5}_{#4}$ = the C ascending melodic minor scale

THE ASCENDING MELODIC MINOR SCALE AND ITS DERIVATIVES

THE SCALE ABOVE CONTAINS THE FOLLOWING:

61

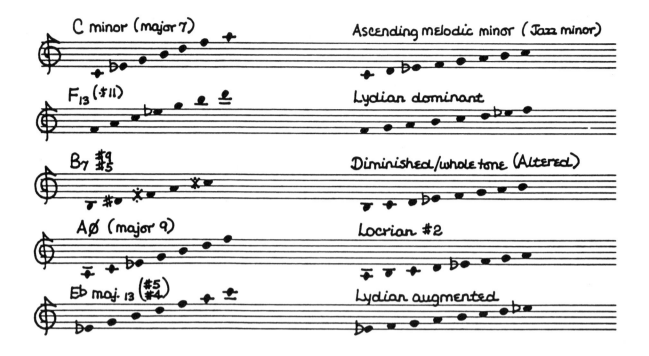

THE WHOLE TONE SCALE

The characteristics of the whole tone scale are as follows:

1. There are only six different tones in any whole tone scale.
2. All adjacent tones are a whole step apart.
3. There are only major thirds and augmented triads in a whole tone scale.
4. There are only two whole tone scales, and the notes in the two are mutually exclusive.
5. Because of the lack of half steps this scale palls very quickly and must be used judiciously.

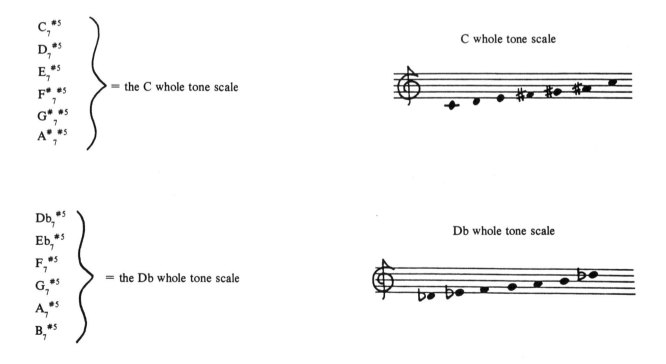

Although there are seemingly crucial notes in conflict with those in the minor seventh chord (II), common practice permits the use of the whole tone scale to color the minor chord. The rule is as follows: use the whole tone scale one half step above the root of the minor seventh chord in question, i.e., Gmi_7 = the Ab whole tone scale.

THE DIMINISHED SCALE

The characteristics of the diminished scale are as follows:

1. There are eight different tones in any diminished scale.
2. The diminished scale consists of alternating half steps and whole steps.
3. All possible chord constructs inherent in the scale duplicate themselves at the interval of the minor 3rd, i.e., the following:

$C_7 \, ^{\#9}_{b9} \, _{b5}$ ------------------- appears at -------------------- $Eb_7 \, ^{\#9}_{b9} \, _{b5}$

C minor$_7$ -------------- appears at ------------------- Eb minor$_7$

$C\emptyset$ ---------------------- appears at -------------------- $Eb\emptyset$

Co ---------------------- appears at ----------------- Ebo

4. There are only three possible diminished scales.
5. This scale is one of the most versatile scales.

$$
\left[
\begin{array}{cccc}
C_7 \, ^{\#9}_{b9}\, _{b5} & Eb_7 \, ^{\#9}_{b9}\, _{b5} & F^{\#}_7 \, ^{\#9}_{b9}\, _{b5} & A_7 \, ^{\#9}_{b9}\, _{b5} \\
Eo_7 & Go_7 & Bbo_7 & Dbo_7 \\
\hline
\multicolumn{4}{c}{\text{(less specific)}} \\
Gmi_7 & Bbmi_7 & Dbmi_7 & Emi_7 \\
G\emptyset & Bb\emptyset & Db\emptyset & E\emptyset
\end{array}
\right]
$$

= C-Db-Eb-E-F#-G-A-Bb-C

RULES: (1) When starting on the root of the seventh chord begin with a half step.

(2) With all other chords, when starting on the root, begin with a whole step.

63

THE DIMINISHED SCALE AND ITS DERIVATIVES

Although there are seemingly crucial scale notes in conflict with those in the minor seventh chord (II) and the half diminished chord (VII), common practice permits the use of the diminished scale over either the II or the VII chord. Over the minor seventh, half diminished seventh, or the diminished seventh, when starting the scale on the tonic of the chord, begin the scale with a whole step.

THE BLUES SCALE

This scale is usually used as a horizontal scale, that is, a scale used to blanket entire areas of a tune as in a blues. The proper scale is determined in two ways: (1) by the key of the music (for example, a blues in F uses an F blues scale, a tune predominantly in the key of F uses an F blues scale, etc.) or (2) the resolving tendencies of two or more chords, i.e., the following example:

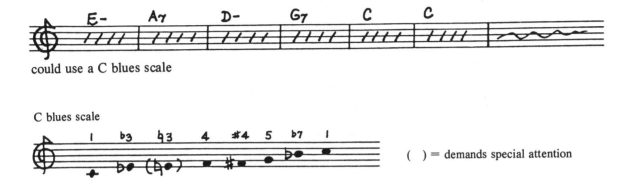

could use a C blues scale

C blues scale

( ) = demands special attention

THE MAJOR PENTATONIC SCALE

The major pentatonic scale consists of the 1-2-3-5-6 notes of a major scale; using the C major scale as an example, the C major pentatonic scale would be C-D-E-G-A. The major pentatonic scale can be used as either a horizontal scale or a vertical scale. When used as a horizontal scale it is usually used to blanket major key areas. As with the blues scale, the scale of the tonic is usually used, i.e., the following:

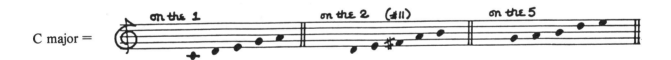

= C major pentatonic

When used as a vertical scale or a scale of high specificity, observe the following rules:

    1. The major chord (I) uses the major pentatonic scale built on the 1, 2, or 5.

C major =

    2. The minor seventh chord (II) uses the major pentatonic scale built on b3, b7, or 4.

D mi$_7$ =

3. The dominant seventh chord (V_7) uses the major pentatonic scale built on 1, 4, b7, b3, b5, or b6.

$G_7 =$

THE MINOR PENTATONIC SCALE

The minor pentatonic scale consists of the 1-b3-4-5-b7 notes of a major scale; using the C major scale as an example, the C minor pentatonic scale would be C-Eb-F-G-Bb. The minor pentatonic scale can be used as either a horizontal scale or a vertical scale. When used as a horizontal scale, the same rules are observed as for the blues scale.

When used as a vertical scale, observe the following rules:

1. The major chord (I) uses the minor pentatonic scale built on the 6, 7, or 3.

C major =

2. The minor seventh chord (II) uses the minor pentatonic scale built on the 1, 5, or 2.

D mi$_7$ =

3. The dominant seventh chord (V_7) uses the minor pentatonic scale built on the 6, 2, 5, 1, b3, or 4.

$G_7 =$

THE BEBOP SCALES (DOMINANT AND MAJOR)

From the early twenties jazz musicians attempted to make their improvised lines flow more smoothly by connecting scales and scale tones through the use of chromatic passing tones. In a detailed analysis of more than 500 solos by the acknowledged giants from Armstrong through Lester Young and Coleman Hawkins, one is aware, first, of the increased use of scales (as opposed to arpeggios and chord outlines) and then the increasing use of chromaticism within these scales. An unusual fact about this increased chromaticism is that, despite the frequent re-occurence of certain licks or patterns, no discernible design with regard to how the extra chromatic tones are added emerges. The overall impression is a somewhat arbitrary or random use of chromaticism.

When one listens to the great players from the distant and near past, one of the main things that tends to "date" their playing (aside from technological improvements in recording techniques, changes with regard to harmonic and rhythmic formulae, etc.) is this lack of unanimity with regard to the use of melodic chromaticism.

From his earliest recordings Charlie Parker can be observed groping for a method for making the modes of the major scale sound less awkward and for rendering them more conducive to swing and forward motion. Gradually, in a systematic and logical way, he began using certain scales with added chromatic tones. Dizzy, approaching the scales from an entirely different direction, began utilizing the same techniques for transforming them. These scales became the backbone of all jazz from bebop to modal music.

A study of a large number of representative solos from the bebop era yields a set of very complex governing rules that have now been internalized and are a part of the language of all good players in the bebop and post-bebop tradition.

Very simply stated, the added chromatic tones make the scales "come out right." Play a descending mixolydian scale and then play the bebop version of the scale and see how much smoother the second scale moves.

There are a number of reasons why the second scale makes more sense. First, in the second scale all of the chord tones are on down beats; and second, the tonic of the scale falls on beat one of each successive measure.

THE BEBOP DOMINANT SCALE

This scale is spelled 1-2-3-4-5-6-b7- ♮7-1 and the rules governing its use are given with the dominant seventh chord as the point of reference. The scale is also used on the related minor seventh chord (II) and, under special conditions to be discussed later, also on the related half diminished seventh chord (VII), i.e. the following:

$$\begin{bmatrix} \text{G-} \\ \text{C}_7 \\ \text{E} \emptyset \text{ (under special conditions)} \end{bmatrix} = \text{C-D-E-F-G-A-Bb-B} \natural \text{ -C}$$

RULES:
1. On a dominant seventh chord the scale is reckoned from the root of the chord, i.e., C_7 = C dominant (bebop)
2. On a minor seventh chord the scale is reckoned from the root of the related dominant seventh chord, i.e., G- = C dominant (bebop)
3. When conditions dictate the use of this scale on a half diminished chord its starting point is reckoned from the root of the related dominant seventh chord, i.e., E∅ = C dominant (bebop)
4. The scale usually moves in basic eighth note patterns.
5. In pure form the scale invariably starts on a down beat.
6. In pure form the scale starts on a chord tone (1, 3, 5, or b7) of the dominant seventh chord.

7. Most often the descending form of the scale is used.

8. As long as the scale starts on a chord tone, the line may ascend in a scalar fashion and return the same way.

9. The line may also descend, then ascend in scalar fashion.

10. When the line starts on the 3rd, it may descend chromatically to the 6th, i.e. the following:

or ascend and then descend chromatically from the 3rd, i.e. the following:

ENDINGS

The endings of phrases are very important, and two particular endings appear with great frequency:

(1)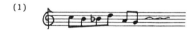

(2)

68

More often than not phrases end on the upbeat of beats one or three, as in the following examples:

(A)

(B)

The line should use whichever of the two endings make this possible.

Please note that in examples #2 and #A the extra half step between the tonic and b7 has been omitted. The rule governing this situation is as follows: if the line is ending, use a whole step as in examples #2 and #A; if the line is to continue, use the half step as usual, as in the following example:

Different endings starting on other chord tones.

STARTING THE SCALE ON NON-CHORD TONES

When starting the scale on a non-chord tone many options exist. Some of the most frequently used ones follow:

1. Use the scale without the extra half step, as in the following examples:

2. Use the scale without the extra half step until you reach the b7, at which time balance is restored and the previous rules are once more operative, as in the following examples:

3. Insert a half step before the first chord tone you come to, as in the following examples:

4. Syncopate the first chord tone you come to, as in the following examples:

5. From the b2 approach the tonic from a half step below, as in the following example:

6. From the b3 approach the 3rd from a half step above, as in the following example:

7. From the #4 descend chromatically to the 3rd, as in the following example:

8. From the b6 approach the 5th from a half step below or ascend chromatically to the b7, as in the following examples:

9. When the line starts with a chord tone on an upbeat, all of the preceeding eight non-chord tone rules are operative since it places a non-chord tone on a down beat.

10. Generally, move by step, half step, or skip until a chord tone occurs on a down beat. All of the preceeding examples exemplify this rule.

EXTENDING THE BEBOP LINE

The bebop dominant scale may be extended through the use of a number of techniques which are a part of the common language of all good jazz musicians. Some of the more common ones follow:

1. Upon arrival on the b7 the line may ascend along a major seventh chord, allowing for extension or change of direction, as in the following examples:

2. Upon arrival on the 3rd, 5th, or b7th, the line may proceed along the outline of the diminished chord containing that note, as in the following example (the diminished chord usually sets up a modulation);

70

Examples A and B may be combined with examples C through H, as in the following example:

3. The bebop line may be extended through the use of what I shall hereafter refer to as deflection. When leaving the 5th of the scale, the line may be deflected in the manner of the following examples (make sure that when the line resumes its descent the 5th is on a down beat):

4. The bebop line may be extended by embellishing the root or the 5th of the chord. This is accomplished by delaying the arrival of the chord tone by inserting the notes one half step above and one half step below the tone in question, as in the following examples:

If the line originates from the 3rd or the b7 rule #4 remains operative, as in the following examples:

If the 3rd is to be embellished within a line, start on the b5, as in the following example:

Or skip from the 4th and return by half step, as in the following example:

These techniques for extending lines are particularly useful in modal situations (as in example #I, which follows), in double time passages where more material is needed to fill the same number of measures (as in example #J, which follows), and simply for variety.

(I)

(J)

71

ACHIEVING VARIETY WITH THE BEBOP DOMINANT SCALES

1. Start the scale on something other than the first beat of the measure, as in the following examples:

2. Vary the starting note (not just the tonic and not just chord tones), as in the following examples:

3. Vary the endings, as in the following examples:

4. Balance ascending and descending motion, as in the following example:

5. Bury the scale within a line, as in the following examples:

6. Turns may be used on any chord tone, as in the following examples:

7. Join bebop scales to other bebop scales, as in the following examples:

8. Join the bebop scales to other scale types, as in the following examples:

9. Use various delays, as in the following examples:

10. Use extensions.

11. Use double time.

USING THE BEBOP DOMINANT SCALE OVER A HALF DIMINISHED CHORD

When the half diminished chord is treated as a minor seventh (II), then all of the aforementioned rules are operative, as exemplified here:

 : use rules for C$_7$

However, if the half diminished chord is perceived as part of a II V$_7$ VII situation (i.e., G-| C$_7$| E⌀ A$_7$| D- as in "Back Home Again in Indiana," "Whisper Not," etc.), then observe the following rule: treat the ⌀ (VII) as the related II V progression, as in the following example:

73

THE BEBOP MAJOR SCALE

The rationale for the use of the bebop major scale is the same as that for the use of the bebop dominant scale. This scale is spelled 1-2-3-4-5-#5-6-7-8 and is used over any major type chord.

RULES: 1. The scale usually moves in basic eighth note patterns and usually descends.

2. In pure form the scale invariably starts on a down beat.

3. In pure form the scale starts on a chord tone. For the purposes of the use of this scale the chord tones are 1, 3, 5, and 6, as in the following example:

4. As long as the scale starts on a chord tone, the line may ascend and/or descend in scalar fashion, as in the following examples:

5. When the scale starts on the 9th, descend chromatically to the major 7th, then observe the basic rule, as in the following examples:

6. When the scale starts on the major 7th, descend chromatically to the 5th of the chord, as in the following examples:

7. When starting on a non-chord tone move by step, half step, or skip until a chord tone (1, 3, 5, or 6) occurs on a down beat.

8. When the solo line starts on a non-chord tone or when the line has a chord tone on an upbeat, insert a half step just before a chord tone to restore balance to the line, as in the following examples:

9. For variety approach the chord tone which initiates the line by a half step above and a half step below, as in the following examples:

74

ACHIEVING VARIETY WITH THE BEBOP MAJOR SCALE

1. Start the scale on something other than the first beat of the measure.
2. Vary the starting note (not just the tonic and not just chord tones).
3. Balance ascending and descending motion.
4. Bury the scale within less obvious lines.
5. Turns may be used on any chord tone, as in the following examples:

The choices of scales to color chords are not entirely arbitrary but are governed by a number of considerations.

Some of these considerations are:

1. The writer's personal taste (one scale sounds better to him than another.)

2. How consonant or dissonant the writer would like the line to be in relation to the chord.

3. Certain alterations in the given chord (**always** choose a scale that takes into consideration alterations in the chord. For example, in a C$_7$ $^{\#9}_{\#5}$ [C-E-G$^\#$-B$^\flat$-D$^\#$] choose a dominant seventh scale that includes a G$^\#$ and a D$^\#$.)

The information in this chapter is based on personal observations of many of the most important jazz players of our time. It is beyond the scope of this chapter to deal with the theoretical concepts that underlie the choices of scales that accompany particular chords. Furthermore, this information should not cause the player to close his mind to the many other scale systems and possibilities for constructing and using his own scales.

When dealing with other scale systems it is perhaps better to adopt the nomenclature and rules of that system. However, settle in your own mind which scales are similar and how they operate in the different systems.

OTHER SCALE CHOICES

The following chart presents other scale possibilities to color specific chord types. Scales start on the name of the chord unless otherwise indicated.

1. **Major Scale Choices**

	Scale Name
C △ (can be written C)	Major (don't emphasize the 4th)
C △ +4	Lydian (major scale with +4)
C △ b6	Harmonic major
C △ +5, +4	Lydian augmented
C	Augmented
C	Diminished (begin with ½ step)
C	Blues scale
C	Major pentatonic
C	Bebop major

2.	**Dominant 7th Scale Choices**		**Scale Name**
	C7	....	Dominant seventh (Mixolydian)
	C7+4	....	Lydian dominant
	C7b6	....	Hindu
	C7+ (has #4 & #5)	....	Whole tone
	C7b9 (also has #9, #4)	....	Diminished (begin with ½ step)
	C7+9 (also has b9, #4, #5)	....	Diminished/whole tone
	C7	....	Blues scale
	C7	....	Major pentatonic
	C7	....	Bebop dominant

3.	**Minor Scale Choices**		**Scale Name**
	C−	....	Minor (Dorian)
	C−b6	....	Pure minor
	C−△ (major seventh)	....	Ascending melodic minor
	C−	....	Blues scale
	C−	....	Diminished (begin with whole step)
	C−△ (b6 & major seventh)	....	Harmonic minor
	C−	....	Phrygian
	C−	....	Minor pentatonic
	C−	....	Bebop dominant starting on F

4.	**Half Diminished Scale Choices**		**Scale Name**
	Cø	....	Half diminished (Locrian)
	Cø	....	Bebop dominant starting on F
	Cø	....	Bebop dominant starting on Ab
	Cø#2	....	Half diminished #2 (Locrian #2)

5.	**Diminished Scale Choice**		**Scale Name**
	Co	....	Diminished

6.	**Dominant 7th Suspended 4th**		**Scale Name**
	C7 sus 4	....	Dominant 7th scale, but don't emphasize the 3rd
	C7 sus 4	....	Major pentatonic starting on Bb
	C7 sus 4	....	Bebop dominant

SUGGESTED READING . . .

Techniques of Improvisation. Volume 1: A Method for Developing Improvisational Technique (Based on the Lydian Chromatic Concept by George Russell) by David Baker

Advanced Improvisation by David Baker. Volume I, chapter 8; Volume II, chapters 7-14.

A New Approach to Ear Training for the Jazz Musician by David Baker

Ear Training for Jazz Musicians. Volume 3: Seventh Chords/Scales by David Baker

The Lydian Chromatic Concept of Tonal Organization for Improvisation by George Russell

Jamey Aebersold series: *A New Approach to Jazz Improvisation. Volume I: A New Approach to Jazz Improvisation. Volume 2: Nothin' But Blues. Volume 21: Gettin' It Together. Volume 24: Major & Minor. Volume 26: The Scale Syllabus.*

The Complete Method for Improvisation by Jerry Coker

Scales for Jazz Improvisation by Dan Haerle

Pentatonic Scales for Jazz Improvisation by Ramon Ricker

Thesaurus of Scales and Melodic Patterns by Nicholas Slonimsky

Encyclopedia of Scales by Don Schaeffer and Charles Colin

Patterns for Saxophone by Oliver Nelson

SUGGESTED LISTENING . . .

Virtually any jazz record with first-class players, arrangers and composers. For an extensive list of recordings using specific scales see *Advanced Improvisation* by David Baker, volume I, chapter 8.

Chapter XI

TWO-VOICE WRITING

In writing for two voices in a jazz idiom, a number of distinct possibilities exist.

1. Parallel writing—the two voices move in parallel motion predominently. The second voice is for all practical purposes a shadow of the top voice. **(example 1)**
2. Polyphonic writing—In this style of writing the second voice does **not** mirror the top voice. The two voices move in oblique or contrary motion and usually avoid rhythmic duplication. This is essentially the classical approach. **(example 2)**
3. Scalar writing—a kind of writing just as easily called modal writing which combines the techniques of parallel and polyphonic writing. **(example 3)**
4. Simple-shell two-horn technique—a technique usually used by two horns accompanying a melodic line. **(example 4)**
5. Lead voice with a bass line. (self explanatory)

Very few compositions lend themselves entirely to a single technique Some general rules that transcend categories then some specific rules follow:

1. 3rds and 6ths are best (consonances).
2. 2nds and 7ths are usable.
3. Tritone used sparingly.
4. 5ths and octaves used only under special circumstances (move in or out of 5ths and octaves).
5. 4ths are bad except to set up tendencies (move in or out of 4ths).
6. When harmonies are extended use secondary chords and resolutions. (II V I substitutions) **(example 5)**
7. Use tendency tones and passing tones. **(example 6)**
8. Try to change harmony part if harmony changes across the bar line. **(example 7)**
9. Use turnback (turnarounds) at ends of sections. (i.e., 1st and 2nd ending or terminal ending.) **(example 8)**
10. Introduce dissonance for reasons of tension. **(example 9)**
11. Avoid harmonizing rest points with 6th of key. **(example 10)**
12. Decide whether 2nd part is to be a bass line or one actual 2nd voice or a mirror of the 1st voice.

I. Parallel Writing

   a. Two voices.
   b. Both voices within the octave.
   c. Avoid crossing.
   d. Second voice usually parallels the motion of the top voice.
   e. Harmony is mostly thirds and sixths.

The harmony note may come from the chord itself if it is one of the chord tones or it may come from the scale to which the chord belongs (dorian, mixolydian, etc.) **(example Ia)**

Pa. W. is a composition harmonized according to this technique.

II. Polyphonic Writing

   a. Two voices.
   b. Both voices within the octave.
   c. Avoid crossings.
   d. Overlap phrases (try to make points of rest different). **(example IIa)**
   e. Free rhythm (but not too complex).
   f. Try to work with just two or three different note values. **(example IIb)**
   g. **Use rests.**
   h. Don't use tritones, minor seconds or major sevenths except as suspensions, delays and for melodic reasons.
   i. Account for basic units of the time. (There must be movement on each unit of the time, i.e., in 4/4 time each quarter note must be accounted for.) **(example IIc)**
   j. Contrary or oblique motion is desirable. **(example IId)**
   k. Use conflicting rhythms whenever possible. **(example IIe)**

    l.   Avoid duplication of figures that divide the time unit. **(example IIf)**

    m.   In general, the second voice is less independent than the first but the rules for melodic construction should still be observed.

    n.   Avoid cross relationships. **(example IIg)**

    o.   The highest and lowest points should not be the same in both voices.

    p.   Avoid chord outlines (tertian, quartal, etc.) **(example IIh)**

Po. W. is a composition harmonized according to this technique.

III. Scalar Writing

    a.   Two horns.

    b.   Both voices within the octave.

    c.   Avoid crossings.

    d.   Motion is parallel, oblique and contrary.

    e.   Choose and adhere to scale colors (i.e., lydian, conventional or other scales). **(example IIIa)**

    f.   Use simple major scales unless the chord dictates otherwise. **(example IIIb)**

    g.   Essentially thirds and sixths.

    h.   Use other intervals discreetly.

    i.   Scalar writing is very often used as an adhesive technique. **(example IIIc)**

    j.   Set tension points. **(example IIId)**

    k.   Set and use rhythmic schemes for cohesion. **(example IIIe)**

S. W. is a composition harmonized according to this technique.

IV. Simple-Shell Technique

    a.   Two voices.

    b.   Both voices within the octave.

    c.   Avoid crossings.

In major chords the second voice usually moves 7 to 6 or within the implied major scale. **(example IVa)**

In minor seventh chords the $^b7$ descends a half step to the sixth of the key (which is the 3rd of the dominant 7th). **(example IVb)**

If the melody is the minor third use the ninth moving within the scale. **(example IVc)** The writer may also operate from within the appropriate dorian scale or another scale if an alteration demands it. **(example IVd)**

Treat the dominant seventh as though it were a minor seventh resolving to a dominant. (Use the above rule.) The writer may also operate with the proper mixolydian scale or another scale which an alteration might demand. **(example IVe)**

With a diminished chord choose another member of the diminished chord or the proper diminished scale. **(example IVf)**

Treat the augmented chord as a dominant seventh chord. **(example IVg)**

    d.   The second voice usually moves with the harmonic rhythm or the implied harmonic rhythm of the tune. **(example IVh)**

    e.   Notes smaller than the basic unit of the time or notes that intersect the basic time may be harmonized in parallel 3rds, 6ths, 4ths. Octaves and unisons may also be used. **(example IVi)**

Remember many compositions don't lend themselves to this technique of harmonization.

S. S. is a composition harmonized according to this technique.

V. Lead Voice With A Bass Line

    a.   Two voices.

    b.   No crossing.

    c.   Bottom voice usually plays roots joined by sliding runs, although higher partials of the chord are often used. **(example Va)** This technique is very limited in its use.

L. V. B. is a composition harmonized according to this technique.

A two-horn arrangement showing a mixture of the techniques follow: **(example mixed)**

SUGGESTED LISTENING . . .

Any Horace Silver Quintet recording

Any Cannonball Adderley Quintet recording

Any Art Blakey Quintet recording

Any recording by the various versions of the Miles Davis Quintet in the 1950s and 1960s

Any recording of the Max Roach-Clifford Brown Quintet

Any J. J. Johnson Quintet recording

Any Wynton Marsalis Quintet recording

Any recording of the Jay and Kai Quintet

SUGGESTED ASSIGNMENTS . . .

1. Study albums involving two horns. Analyze according to the techniques described in this chapter.
2. Write arrangements using each of the techniques.
3. Write arrangements combining the techniques.

Two-voice Writing (Examples)

82

April B

J Is For Loveliness

Passion

The Dude

Repeat 1st 8 measures (with 2nd ending)

Treat the half-diminished chord as a minor 7th

Treat the minor 6th (tonic minor) as a minor 7th but use a major 7th
instead of a ♭7 in all cases.

88

Dominant 7th

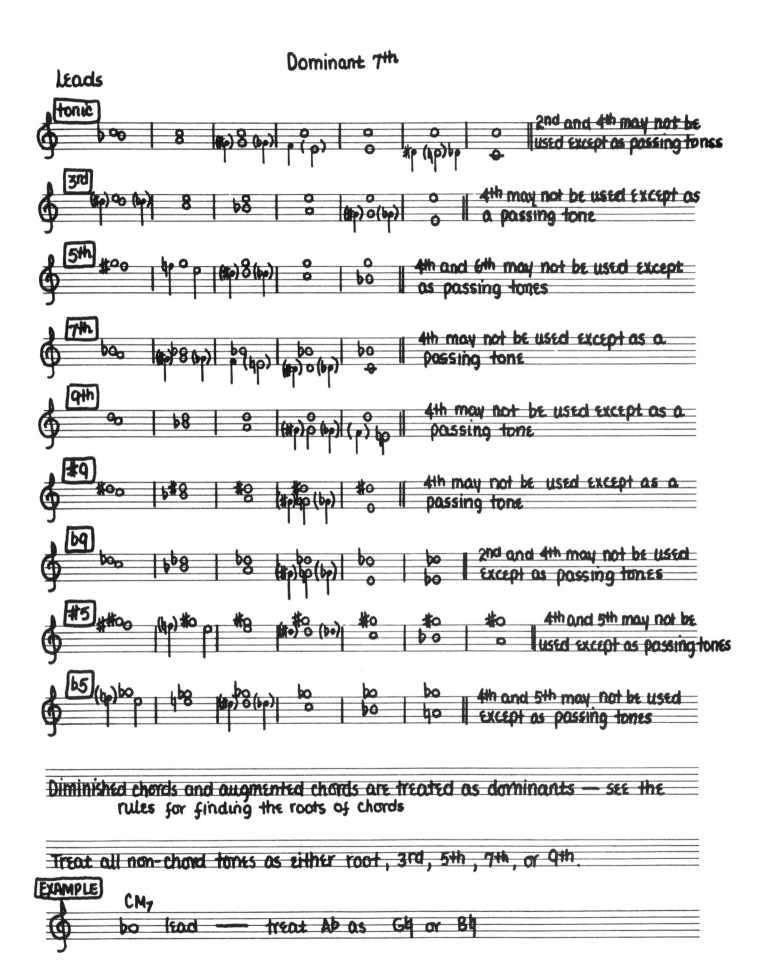

Diminished chords and augmented chords are treated as dominants — see the rules for finding the roots of chords

Treat all non-chord tones as either root, 3rd, 5th, 7th, or 9th.

EXAMPLE

CM₇

bo lead — treat Ab as G# or B♮

Chapter XII

TURNBACKS

The term turnback usually refers to a two-measure progression consisting of four chords. This progression serves a number of purposes. First, it helps define the form of a composition. For instance, in a blues the last two measures of each chorus consists of a I chord. The first four measures also consists of a I chord; consequently, the listener hears six measures of a tonic chord. These six measures could be divided 1 + 5, 5 + 1, 4 + 2, 2 + 4 or 3 + 3. By using the turnback the performer is able to clearly indicate the correct division 2 + 4. Secondly, it serves the purpose of providing a link from one chorus to another. A third purpose served is that of preventing staticness. For example, it provides the possibility for harmonic motion where no motion exists. A fourth purpose served is that of providing rhythmic and melodic interest at the ends of sections within compositions.

The writer may introduce one of the turnback patterns when:

1. The composition calls for that specific progression.

Example

Dmi$_7$	G$_7$	CM$_7$	E^b	A^b	D^b
/ / / /	/ / / /	/ /	/ /	/ /	/ /

2. The last two measures of one section of a tune consists of a tonic chord and the first beat of the next section is also a tonic chord. (The tonic chord may be major or minor.)

Example

Dmi$_7$	G$_7$	Fmi$_7$	B$^b_7$	CM$_7$	CM$_7$ ‖	CM$_7$
/ / / /	/ / / /	/ / / /	/ / / /	/ / / /	/ / / / ‖	/ / / /
				C E^b	A^b D^b ‖	C

└——Substitute——┘

OR

Emi$_7$	A$_7$	DM$_7$	DM$_7$	DM$_7$	G$_7$	CM$_7$	CM$_7$
/ / / /	/ / / /	/ / / /	/ / / /	/ / / /	/ / / /	/ / / /	/ / / /
		D C	B^b E^b			C E^b	A^b D^b

The combination of the turnback with the II V$_7$ progression comprises one of the most important formulae in jazz. The ability to cope with turnbacks make the writer's task infinitely easier.

Virtually every composition written in the jazz and pop idioms can be enlivened and made more interesting by the interjection of well-placed turnbacks. This chapter includes a number of turnback formulae.

SUGGESTED ASSIGNMENTS . . .

1. Locate five records that include turnbacks and write down the formulae.
2. Find at least five tunes that contain potential turnbacks within the tune (not as the final two measures).
3. Be able to write at least three different turnback formulae in any key, tempo or meter.

Turnback Formulae

① I: CM7 bIII: EbM7 / Eb7 bVI: AbM7 bII: DbM7 / Db7 I: C

② I: CM7 bVII: BbM7 / Bb7 bIII: EbM7 bII: DbM7 / Db7 I: C

③ I: CM7 bVII: BbM7 bVI: AbM7 bII: DbM7 / Db7 I: C

④ I: CM7 bIII: EbM7 / Eb7 II: DM7 / D7 bII: DbM7 / Db7 I: C

⑤ I: CM7 VI: AM7 / A7 bV: GbM7 / Gb7 bIII: EbM7 / Eb7 I: C

⑥ I: CM7 bIII: EbM7 / Eb7 bV: GbM7 / Gb7 VI: AM7 / A7 I: C

⑦ I: CM7 IV: FM7 / Fmi7 bIII: EbM7 / Ebmi7 bII: DbM7 / Dbmi7 / Db7 I: C

⑧ I: CM7 VI: Ami7 II: Dmi7 V: G7 I: C

⑨ I: CM7 VI: Ami7 / A7 bVI: Abmi7 / Ab7 V: G7 I: C

⑩ I: CM7 VI: Ami7 bVI: Abmi7 bII: Db7 I: C

⑪ I: CM7 bVII: BbM7 II: Dmi7 bII: Db7 I: C

⑫ I: CM7 bVII: BbM7 II: Dmi7 V: G7 I: C

91

Chords are interchangeable with other chords in the same column.

Chapter XIII

THREE-VOICE WRITING

The technique of three-voice parallel writing carries with it certain rules as did two-voice writing but the three-voice variety tends to be much more rewarding. The addition of a third voice opens up many more possibilities.

The rules for three-voice writing follow:

1. Three voices all within an octave.
2. Avoid the use of the perfect fourth above the root of the given chord except as a passing tone or embellishing tone.
3. The bottom voices may move freely within the major key area or within the area of the chosen scale. **(example 1)** Chromaticism is also possible. **(example 2)**
4. Avoid the use of triads whenever possible.
   a. Try to introduce dissonance between two of the voices. **(example 3)**
   b. Triads are feasible when one or more of the voices provides a contextual dissonance. (example: C triad over a D minor 7th chord.) The note C provides the dissonant interval of a seventh above the note D.
5. The basic notes in major chords are the upper extension 6 - 7 - 9 - 11 - 13. In the major chord the major 7th against the tonic is very effective. **(example 4)**
6. The basic notes in a minor 7th to dominant 7th situation are still the ^{b}7 of the minor chord resolving down a half step. **(example 5)**
7. If the II is given, supply the V_7. **(example 6)**
   If the V_7 is given, supply the II. **(example 7)**
8. Harmonize with duplicate movement or by use of two-voice harmony in the bottom two voices. **(example 8)**
9. The use of perfect fourths can provide variety and color. All 4ths must be contained in the major scale to which the given chord belongs. **(example 9)** Exception—you may use a pair of 4ths containing the raised 4th of the major scale to which the given chord belongs. **(example 10)**
10. When desired examine the possibility for the use of a "blues" voicing. **(example 11)**
11. If the melody is static you may move the bottom two voices in parallel thirds, fourths or seconds. **(example 12)**
12. Try whenever possible for contrary motion between the top voice and the bottom pair. **(example 13)**
13. At points of rest (cadences, etc.) two or all three voices may move freely. **(example 14)**
14. In modal compositions triads may be used freely.

    Dahomey Dance . . . . Coltrane
    Milestones . . . . Miles Davis
    So What . . . . Miles Davis
    Freddie the Freeloader . . . . Miles Davis

15. Treat non-chord tones as chord tones, **(example 15)**, or as members of one of the scales to which the chord belongs. **(example 16)**

THREE-HORN ARRANGEMENTS ARE INCLUDED

A three-horn voicing chart follows on pages 96-97. It should be used in the following manner:
   a. Determine the quality of the chord you want to voice (major, minor, dominant, etc.)
   b. Determine the member of the chord that is in the lead (1, 3, 5, 7, 9, etc.)
   c. Check the chart for the corresponding set-up.
   d. Choose one of the voicings that satisfies the aesthetic demands of the musical situation.

SUGGESTED LISTENING . . .

Any recording of the Miles Davis Sextet from the early 1950s (with J. J. Johnson and Jimmy Heath)
Any recording of the Miles Davis Sextet with Cannonball Adderley and John Coltrane
Any J. J. Johnson Sextet recording
Any Jazztet recording

Any George Russell Sextet recording
Any Art Blakey Sextet recording
Curtis Fuller: *Sliding Easy* (United Artists UAL 4041)

SUGGESTED ASSIGNMENTS . . .

1. Listen to and analyze three-horn compositions by your favorite writers.
2. Score some compositions of your own choosing for three horns using both the techniques described in this chapter and the three-horn chart.

Three-Voice Writing

Three-voice Writing Chart
Minor 7th

Gmi
I
(F to E is the resolution)   3rd

Either of the bottom two notes moves toward the 3rd or 7th of the dominant.

5th

7th

Leads

Dominant 7th

①

③

⑤

⑦

⑨

#5   Triad major 3rd above

b5   Triad a step above

b9

Triad 6th above

Major

Triad minor 6th above

Any movement of single notes or 3rds within the scale except the 4th.

Ex.

any movement within the scale

C + Bmajor triad | D major triad | Gb triad

In all the preceeding examples, treat the non-chord as one of these:
root, 3rd, 5th, 7th, or 9th

97

Passion

Repeat 1st 8 measures (with 1st ending)

unison with trpt.

unison with trpt.

pizz

99

J Is For Loveliness

100

Chapter XIV

FOUR-VOICE WRITING

The following rules should be observed in scoring for four voices moving in parallel fashion.

1. There must be four **different** voices. (Unlike choral writing in which one voice is doubled.) **(example 1)**
2. All four voices must be within an octave. **(example 2)**
3. Each family of chords reacts differently.
4. Major chords.
   a. Add major 6, 7 or 9 (usually in that order) to the basic triad to obtain a fourth voice. **(example 3)** If the lead voice is an extension you may voice down the chord heading for the tonic. Example:

9	or	11
7		9
5		7
3		5

   b. It is also possible to use different combinations of the degrees of the major scale to which the chord in question belongs, (1, 2, 3, 5, 6, 7) excepting the perfect fourth. **(example 4)**
   c. You may also use combinations involving the raised eleventh or raised fourth. **(example 5)**
   d. Some moving voice possibilities in this category include 7 - 6 or other diatonic movement including + 4 or 9 to 1 if anything but the root of the chord is in the lead. **(example 6)**
5. Minor seventh chords.
   a. All four notes are already present.
   b. All four voices must be within the octave.
   c. There must be four **different** voices.
   d. When necessary or for variety add major ninth, perfect eleventh or major seventh. **(example 7)**
   e. Other combinations of 1, 2, ♭3, 4, 5, 6, ♭7, ♮7 may be used. **(example 8)**
   f. Dorian diatonicism may be used freely (i.e., Dmi₇ chord may draw from the notes of a D dorian scale). **(example 9)**
   g. Other scale possibilities may be used according to chord alterations or personal taste. **(example 10)**
   h. Particularly effective movement in the minor 7th chord. **(example 11)**
6. Dominant seventh.
   a. There must be four **different** voices.
   b. All four voices must be within the octave.
   c. The third and seventh should be present whenever possible.
   d. Don't use a plain dominant seventh, that is, a dominant seventh chord with no altered notes and no added notes. **(example 12)**
   e. Any movement is permissable within the mixolydian scale or another predetermined scale of your choice. **(example 13)**
   f. To avoid a plain dominant seventh add some form of the ninth if anything but the root of the chord is in the lead. **(example 14)**
   g. If the root of the chord is in the lead alter the fifth. **(example 15)**
   h. If the ninth is the lead, the root may be omitted. **(example 16)**
   i. The fifth and the ninth are the two notes normally altered in a dominant seventh chord. **(example 17)**
   j. For variety or added color add any combination of the following:

9	6	(♯4)	♯5
♭9			
♯9	♭6		♭5

   (example 18)

   k. Treat diminished chords as derived dominant sevenths. (A diminished chord is a dominant seventh with a flat nine e g b♭ d♭.) Refer to rule in nomenclature chapter. **(example 19)**
   l. Treat augmented chords as dominant seventh chords of the same name. **(example 20)**
7. Half diminished chords (∅7 or minor 7th ♭5) are treated as minor seventh chords. **(example 21)**
8. When the minor chord functions as a tonic chord (I) add the sixth or the major seventh. **(example 22)** If you add the minor 7th it then implies motion because the resultant chord sound is that of II (minor 7th) moving to V₇ (dominant).

9. Treat non-chord tones as chord tones **(example 23)** or as members of one of the scales to which the chord belongs. **(example 24)**
10. For variety, smoother line and change of color, skips in the melody or less often in other parts may be joined by using scale runs. (See Chapter X for determining what scales color what chords.) **(example 25)**
11. Once the melody note has sounded at the end of a phrase or other point of rest, composed melodies drawn from scales or other sources may be employed to relieve the staticness. **(example 26)**
12. In four voice writing it is often possible to employ certain formulae in the various endings of A A B A compositions. **(example 27)**
13. Often it is desirable to drop the second voice (from the top) in the four voice construct. The resultant voicing is one of the most popular and the most frequently used voicings in modern writing. It is used when:
    a. A closed or tight voicing would force the bottom voice into an unnaturally high or uncomfortable register. **(example 28)**
    b. Variety is desired. **(example 29)**
14. The closed voicing technique may be interchanged freely with the dropped voice technique. **(example 30)**
15. The voicing chart (pages 105-108) should be used in this manner:
    a. Determine the quality of the chord you want to voice (major, minor, dominant, etc.)
    b. Determine what member of the chord is in the lead (1, 3, 5, 7, 9, etc.)
    c. Check the chart for the corresponding set-up.
    d. Choose one of the voicings that satisfies the aesthetic demands of the situation. The chords with the most congestion are usually the most dissonant. **(example 31)**

SUGGESTED LISTENING . . .

Any recording of the Four Freshmen

Any recording of the HiLos

David Baker's 21st Century Bebop Band: *R.S.V.P.* (Laurel Record LR-504)

David Baker's 21st Century Bebop Band: *Struttin'* (Laurel Record LR-505)

SUGGESTED ASSIGNMENTS . . .

1. Listen to and analyze some four-horn compositions by your favorite writers.
2. Score some compositions of your own choosing (both swing and ballads) for four horns using both the techniques described in this chapter and the four-horn chart.

4 Voice Writing (Examples)

Four-voice Writing Chart

105

Dominant 7th

106

107

#5 lead — same as 5 ; omit voicings which contain the #5 in the lower 3 notes.

b5 lead — same as 5 ; omit voicings which contain the b5 in the lower 3 notes.

#9 lead }
b9 lead } — same as 9 ; omit voicings in which one of the lower 3 notes is the same as the lead note.

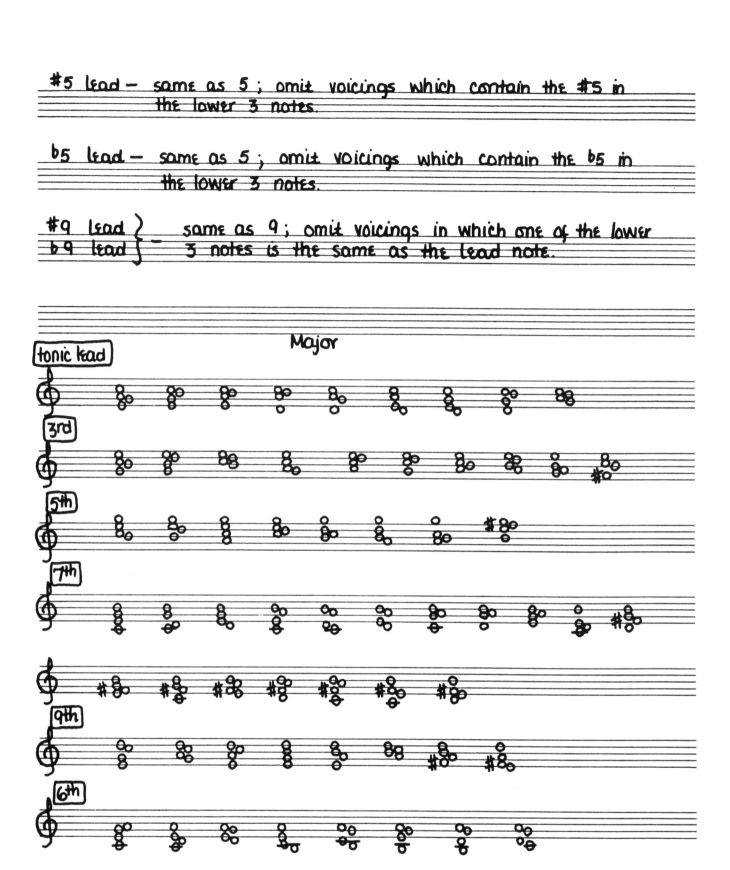

Major

Arranger—Composer: DAVID N. BAKER

Composition : CAHAPHi

♩=152

Composition: CAHAPHi

Arranger-Composer: DAVID N. BAKER

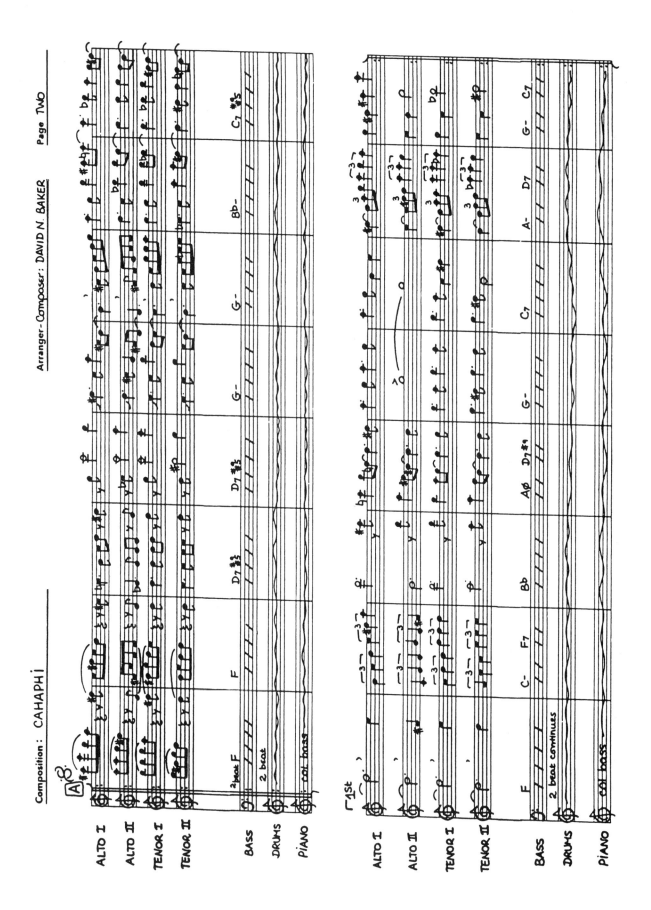

Composition : CAHAPHI   Arranger-Composer : DAVID N. BAKER   Page THREE

Composition: CAHAPHi

Arranger-Composer: DAVID N. BAKER

Page FOUR

112

Chapter XV

FIVE-VOICE WRITING

There are a number of ways to obtain a fifth voice in parallel jazz scoring. One is to simply double the lead voice an octave lower. **(example 1)**

Another way is to write **low roots** in the bass part. With this technique, obviously, the rule about all voices being within an octave is waived. Some times the bass note will merely be a duplication of one of the upper voices; at other times it will be a new voice. **(example 2)**

Both of the above techniques are often used with the dropped voice described in four-voice writing.

While the aforementioned techniques are useful, practical and necessary, we will use the term five-voice writing to refer to a technique utilizing five **different** voices. The rules for this technique follow:

1. There must be five **different** voices.
2. All five voices must be within an octave.
3. Account for all of the chord tones. Then choose the fifth tone from the remaining tones of the implied major scale. In the case of altered chords or for variety, the notes may be chosen from some other predetermined scale. **(example 3)**
4. In general the rules for four-voice writing pertain to five-voice writing.
5. The voicing chart (pages 116-118) should be used in the following manner:
   a. Determine the quality of the chord you want to voice (major, minor, dominant, etc.)
   b. Determine what member of the chord is in the lead (1, 3, 5, 7, 9, etc.)
   c. Check the chart for the corresponding set-up.
   d. Choose one of the voicings that satisfies the aesthetic demands of the situation.

Background five-voice writing. A special situation arises when the five voices comprise the background to a solo line (vocal or instrumental). It is still possible to write the background according to the five-voice rules or the five-voice chart but it is often desirable to use the chart on page 115.

The main advantage to this voicing is its flexibility. The voicing affords twelve possibilities with minimum effort and movement. There are six possibilities with the II to V_7 root movement and six more possibilities with the II to ^{b}II root movement.

SUGGESTED LISTENING . . .

Listen to the saxophone section in any good big band.

Listen to any recording of Supersax.

SUGGESTED ASSIGNMENTS . . .

1. Listen and analyze some compositions by your favorite writers. Try to discover the different approaches described in this chapter.
2. Write some exercises of five-voice writing (4 voices with a double lead).
3. Write some exercises of five-voice writing (4 voices with low roots).
4. Write some exercises with five different voices.
5. Write examples of numbers 2, 3, and 4 with a dropped second voice.
6. Write some exercises using the background writing technique.
   a. Vocal backgrounds, both ballads and swing tunes.
   b. Instrumental backgrounds to an improvised solo.

Five - voice Writing

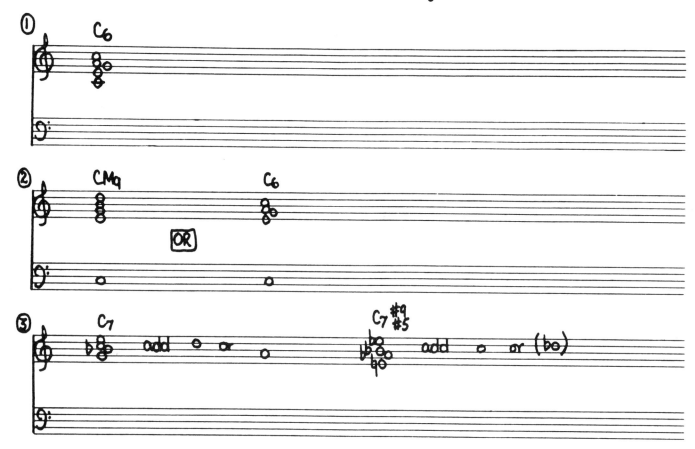

Backrounds - Five voices

Five-voice Writing Chart
Major

Minor (tonic)

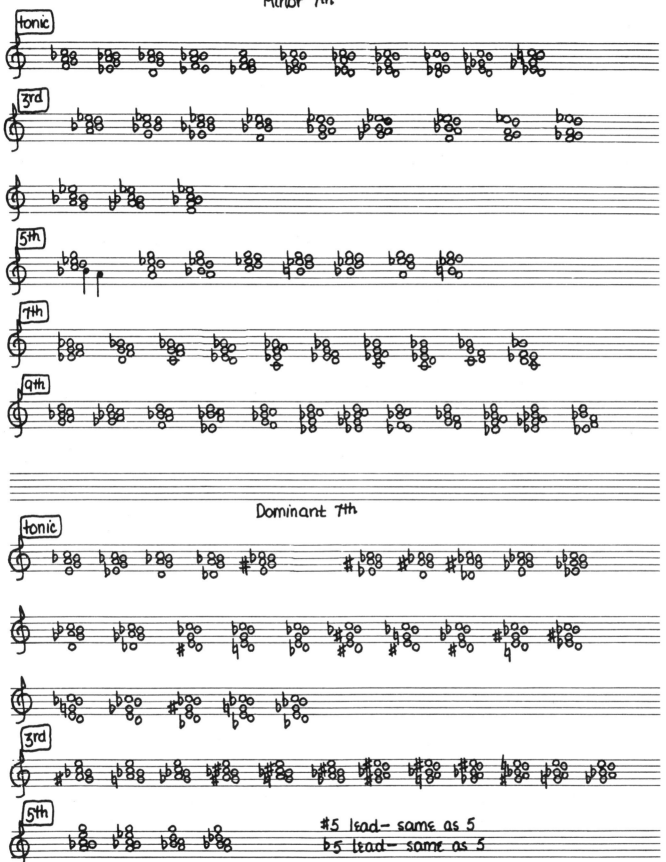

5 horn writing

April B (1st 8 measures)

118

119

5 horn writing   Le Chat Qui Peche (Introduction)

120

Composition and Arrangement Using Scales
Lydian April

5 saxes

121

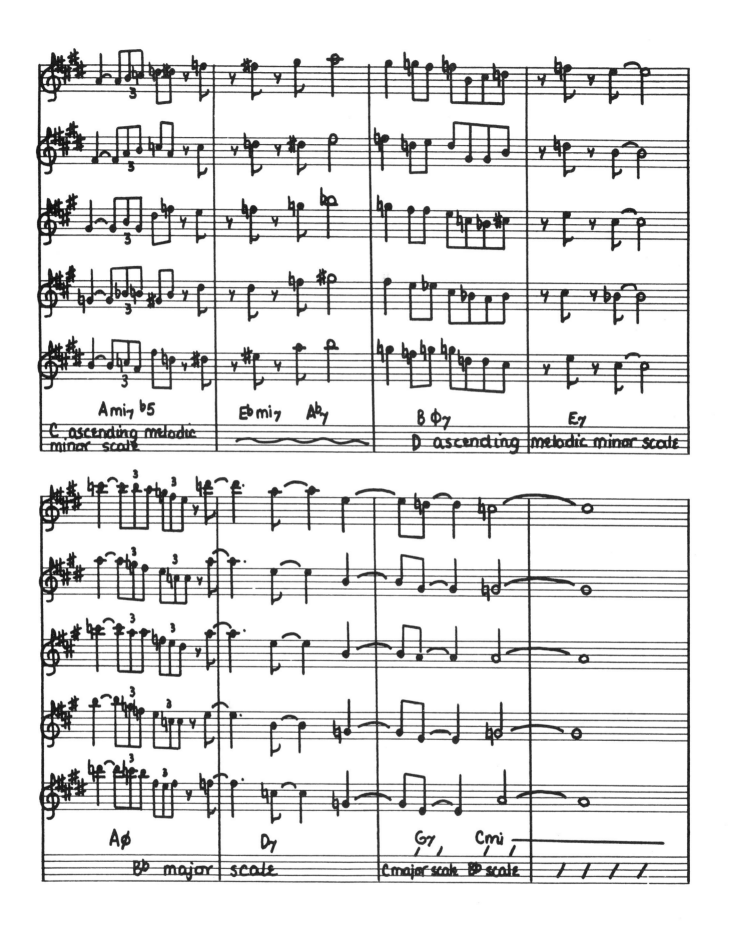

Chapter XVI

SIX-VOICE WRITING

One way to obtain six parts in jazz scoring of a parallel nature without using six different voices is to double the lead voice and add the low roots. **(example 1)** This is a very much-used technique.

To arrive at six **different** voices observe the following rules:

1. There must be six **different** voices.
2. All six voices must be within the octave.
3. First, account for all chord tones. Then choose the remaining two tones from the implied major scale. In case of altered chords or for variety the remaining notes may be chosen from some other predetermined scale. **(example 2)**
4. In general the rules for four-voice writing pertain to six-voice writing.
5. Very often in six-voice writing the second and fourth voice from the top are dropped an octave. **(example 3)**

From five voices upward (6, 7, 8, etc.), the chances for varying tension from chord to chord lessen considerably. One of the reasons is that with five or more voices, all of the notes of the implied scale are present in every chord. This uniformity of tension gives the illusion of staticness or lack of forward motion. For this reason it is probably better to use this technique sparingly.

The six-voice technique is particularly successful when combined with bitonal writing.

Because of the uniformity of tension when dealing with six notes, the chord chart is omitted.

SUGGESTED LISTENING . . .

Miles Davis: *Birth of the Cool* (Capitol T 762)

Miles Davis: *Miles Davis and His Tuba Band* (Jazz Live BLJ8003)

SUGGESTED ASSIGNMENTS . . .

1. Listen and analyze some six-horn compositions by your favorite writers.
2. Score some compositions of your own choosing (both swing and ballads) for six horns using the techniques described in this chapter.

Six-voice writing

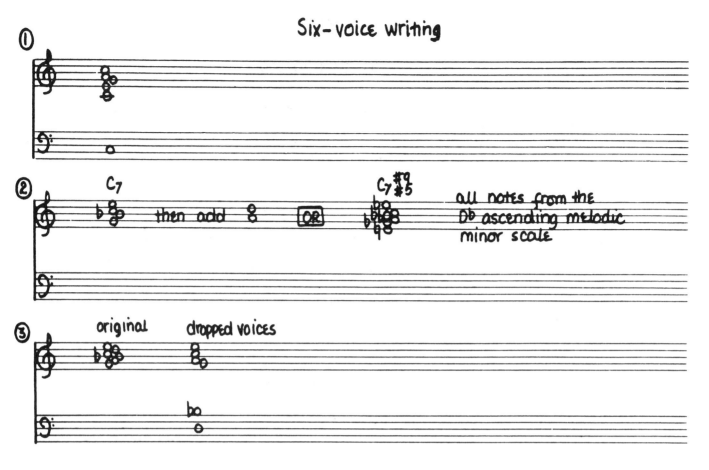

② C7 ... then add ... OR ... C7 #9 #5 ... all notes from the Db ascending melodic minor scale

③ original ... dropped voices

J Is For Loveliness (6 way voicing)

ETC.

Chapter XVII

BITONAL WRITING

Bitonal writing refers to the practice of super-imposing one chord on another. Each class of chords has a different set of bitonal possibilities.

The bitonal chords are most frequently used on the dominant seventh chord. Observe the following rules when the bitonal is comprised of a major triad and a dominant seventh chord.

1. Two different chords. **(example 1)**
2. Five or six voices. **(example 2)**
3. Top three voices make a major triad. (The melody is the root, third or fifth of some major triad.) **(example 3)**
4. If three voices are used on the bottom, the voicing should be 1 ♭7 10. If two voices, use the 3 and the ♭7. **(example 4)**
5. The melody note must not be a perfect fourth or a major seventh above the root of the dominant seventh chord. **(example 5)**
6. If the melody note is a perfect fourth or a major seventh above the root of the dominant seventh which is called for, then a substitute dominant seventh must be used.
   a. Use the dominant seventh chord a minor third or a major sixth above the root of the original dominant seventh chord. **(example 6)**
   b. Substitute dominant seventh chords may also be used for other reasons such as obtaining a better or different bass line **(example 7)**, for variety **(example 8)**, in order to obtain more or less intensity, **(example 9)** or for sheer shock value.
7. The following major triads work as bitonals above a dominant seventh chord. (All triads may be played in any inversion.)

	Whole step above
Dominant 7th	Minor third above
(example 10)	Tri-tone above
	Major or minor sixth above

The following minor triads work as bitonals with the dominant seventh chord. (Triads may be played in any inversion.)

	Triad with the same name
	Perfect 5th above
	½ step above
Dominant 7th	Major 6th above
(example 11)	Tri-tone
	Step above
	Minor 7th above
	Minor 3rd above

The following augmented triads in any inversion:

Dominant 7th	Same name
(example 12)	Step above

The following diminished seventh chords in any inversion:

	Same name
Dominant 7th	♭3
(example 13)	♭5 or 6

8. The Major triad takes the following bitonals:

Major triad + Major triad in any inversion:

	½ step above
	Step above
	Tri-tone
Major triad	Perfect 5th above
(example 14)	Minor 6th above
	Major 6th above
	Major 7th above

125

Major triad + minor triad in any inversion:

	Minor
	Major 3rd above
Major triad	Perfect 5th above
(example 15)	Major 6th above
	Major 7th above

Major triad + augmented triad with all inversions:

Major triad	Augmented
(example 16)	Whole step

Major triad + diminished seventh and all inversions:

	Diminished 7th
Major triad	Same name and inversions
(example 17)	½ step above and inversions

9. The minor triad takes the following bitonals:

Minor triad + Major triad

	Major
	Step above
Minor triad	Minor 3rd above
(example 18)	Perfect 5th above
	Minor 7th above
	Major 7th above

Minor triad + minor triad

	Minor
Minor triad	Step above
(example 19)	Perfect 5th above

Minor triad + augmented triad

Minor (example 20)	Minor 3rd and inversions

Minor triad + diminished 7th

Minor	Diminished 7th
(example 21)	Same name and inversions

10. The augmented triad takes the following bitonals:

Augmented + Major

	Major
	Same name
	Step above
Augmented	Minor 3rd above
(example 22)	Major 3rd above
	Tri-tone
	Minor 6th above
	Major 7th above

Augmented + Minor

	Minor
Augmented	Minor 3rd above
(example 23)	Minor 6th above
	Major 7th above

Augmented + Augmented

Augmented	Augmented
(example 24)	Step above and inversions

Augmented + Diminished 7th

Augmented	Diminished
(example 25)	Step above and inversions

11. The Major 7th chord takes the following bitonals:

Major 7th + Major triads

Major 7th	Step above
(example 26)	Major 3rd above
	Tri-tone
	Perfect 5th above
	Major 6th above
	Major 7th above

Major 7th + Minor triad

Major 7th	Major 3rd above
(example 27)	Major 6th above
	Major 7th above

Major 7th + Augmented triad

Major 7th (example 28)	Same name and all inversions

Major 7th + Diminished 7th chord

Major 7th (example 29)	Same name and all inversions

12. The minor 7th chord takes the following bitonals:

Minor 7th + Major triads

Minor 7th	Major
(example 30)	Step above
	Perfect 4th above
	Perfect 5th above
	Major 6th above
	Minor 7th above

Minor 7th + Minor triad

Minor 7th	Minor
(example 31)	Step above
	Perfect 5th above

Minor 7th + Augmented triad

Minor 7th (example 32)	½ step above and inversions

Minor 7th + Diminished 7th

Minor 7th	Diminished
(example 33)	Same name and inversion
	½ step above

13. The Diminished 7th chord takes the following bitonals:

Diminished 7th + Major triad

Diminished	Major
(example 34)	Step above
	Perfect 4th above
	Major 6th above
	Major 7th above

Diminished 7th + Minor triad

Diminished	Minor
(example 35)	Step above
	Perfect 4th

Diminished + Augmented triad with all inversions

Diminished	Same name
(example 36)	½ step above
	Minor 3rd above

Diminished + any other diminished

14. The half-diminished 7th chord takes the following bitonals:
Half-diminished 7th chord + Major triad

	Major
	½ step above
Half-diminished	Perfect 4th above
(example 37)	Tri-tone
	Minor 6th above
	Minor 7th above

Half-diminished 7th chord + Minor triad

	Minor
	Step above
Half-diminished	Minor 3rd above
(example 38)	Perfect 4th above
	Minor 7th above

Half-diminished 7th chord + Augmented triad

Half-diminished	Augmented
(example 39)	Step above and all inversions

Half-diminished 7th chord + diminished 7th

Half-diminished **(example 40)**	Same name and all inversions

15. Bitonals tend to be most effective when two triads are scored in two different colors.

Top triad	Strings or woodwinds
Bottom chord	Woodwinds or brass
Open Brass	Muted Brass

For this reason it is perhaps better to view chord superimpositions as bitonals rather than extensions or added tones.

J Is For Loveliness (bitonal writing)

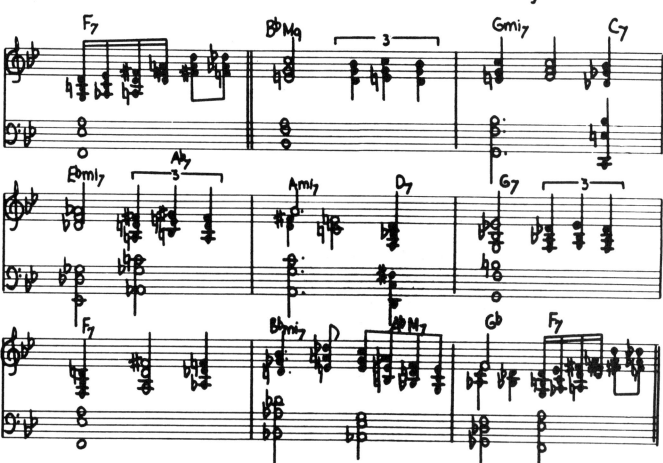

128

Bitonal Writing

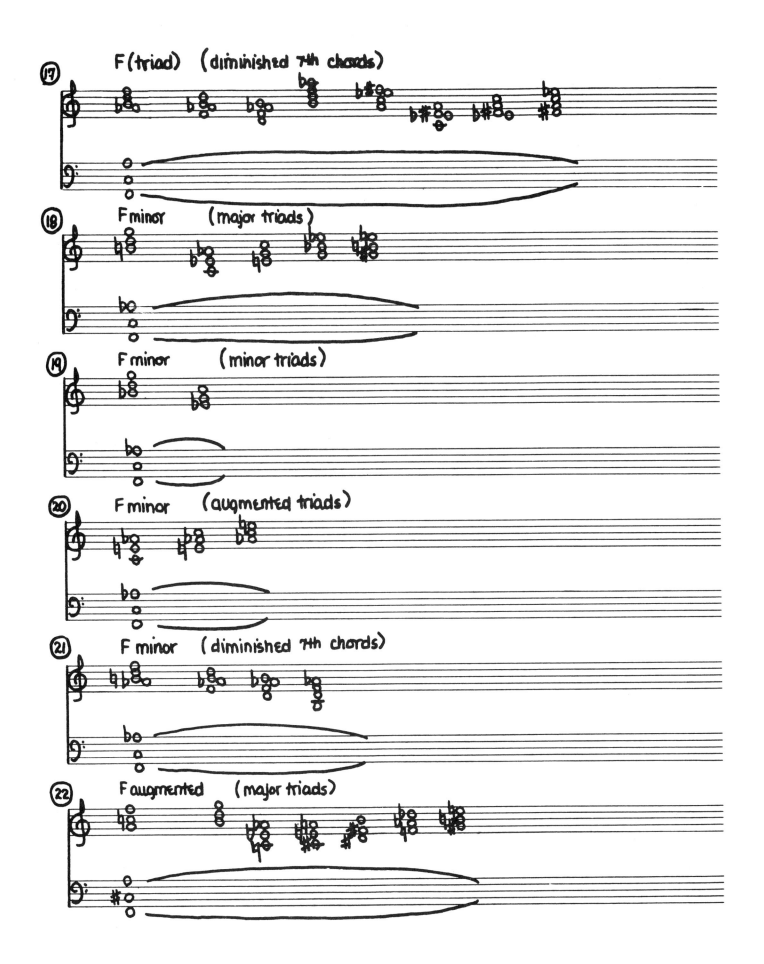

134

Chapter XVIII

PUTTING AN ARRANGEMENT TOGETHER

Once all of the tools of arranging have been acquired then the real tasks begin. How to put the arrangement together?

1. Some considerations include type of group.
   a. abilities
   b. ranges
   c. experience, etc.
2. What kind of piece is it? Ballad, swing tune, stylized type (boogaloo, Latin, etc.)
3. What style of scoring is suggested? (Rely on past experience, records, etc.)
4. What instrumentation are you writing for?
5. What instruments are best suited to play what parts from the standpoint of range, technical capabilities, line suitability, etc.?
6. How many choruses will the piece be? What balance of written arrangement and improvisation? What about backgrounds? Will there be an introduction, interludes? What kind of ending?
7. How will contrast be achieved?

What does the kind of piece have to do with our handling of the scorings? Each tune type by its definition demands certain generalized types of treatment. For instance, a ballad by definition is slow, so harmonies can move faster, lush harmonies might be in order, etc. If the tune is a bebop tune, traditional treatment of bebop tunes should be considered, i.e., melody lines were often stated in unison, lots of substitution, stark harmonies, etc. If the tune is a boogaloo the beat or rhythm is predetermined, an approximate tempo is known, it will probably be relatively simple, etc.

What style of scoring is suggested? If the tune is a quiet ballad don't score the trumpet in its high tessitura ff. Calypso tunes ask for a brass treatment traditionally. Rhythm & blues tunes might suggest electric bass and electric piano.

What instrumentation are you writing for? Check out transposition, ranges, capabilities, etc., of the instruments.

What instruments are best suited to play what parts from the standpoint of range, technical capabilities, for suitability, etc.? Certain keys are better for some instruments than others. i.e., sharp keys are better for strings including violin, flat keys better for winds. Make sure an instrument chosen to play a given line can play the line through its entirety. Assign melodies idiomatically. Give brassy percussive figures to either brass group or brass-led combination. A long scalar line at a fast tempo might be better suited for saxophone than trombone, etc.

Determine ahead of time how many choruses the arrangement has. This allows you to set climaxes, control tension and decide how many choruses soloists will play, placement of backgrounds, etc. A balance between written material and improvised solos must be struck so that the arrangement doesn't sound like a string of solos with a handle on each end. Will there be an introduction? If so, where will the material come from?

The writer may draw material from a number of sources.

1. The theme itself, or some readily discernible element from the melody or rhythm of the composition. This element might then be developed according to the techniques described in the chapter "Developing A Melody."
2. Originally composed material. The original material will probably relate to the composition in one of a number of ways.
   a. The original material might use some aspect of the harmonic scheme of the tune or use the mood of the tune, or it might contrast the mood of the tune.
   b. The original material might be completely unrelated to the tune itself except for tempo or key.
3. Material from another similar tune, (same mood, key, tempo, rhythm, etc.)
4. If it's a show tune, an excerpt from another tune in the same show. ("Summertime" might use a fragment of "It Ain't Necessarily So".) Listen to the Gil Evans-Miles Davis version of "It Ain't Necessarily So," which uses the bridge of "I Got Plenty of Nuthin' " for an introduction.
5. The material might come from a tune with the same words in the title, i.e., "It Might As Well Be Spring," might use the title line from "Spring Will Be A Little Late This Year," or "Spring Can Really Hang You Up The Most," etc.
6. Some figuration or accompaniment figure from the arrangement itself might serve as introduction.

7. A section of the tune might serve as an introduction as usually happens with church hymns and patriotic tunes in which case the last four measures of the tune serves as an introduction. Often a writer will use the bridge of a composition as an introduction.
8. Often a writer will simply reharmonize the melody or a section of the melody and let that serve as an introduction. This technique is often combined with rubato or the use of a meter or tempo other than which the actual tempo or meter of the tune.
9. "Vamps" may also serve as introductions. The vamp is usually a chord pattern executed over a pedal point. The pedal is usually the dominant or the tonic of the key. The number of chords is usually quite limited (between two and five). The chords may be diatonic chords from the key, chromatic chords, mixtures or a harmonized melodic fragment. The vamp is usually quite rhythmic and is often harmonically striking.
10. Introductions are of no set length but traditionally they have been four, eight or sixteen measures long according to tempo, meter, amount of tension desired, etc. The last chord of the introduction should lead into the first chord of the composition. In most instances this merely means the last chord of the introduction will be a dominant seventh of the key, but if the tune starts on a chord other than the tonic, then use a V_7 of that chord.

Remember, the introduction should stimulate the interest of the listener.

Interludes serve a number of purposes. They provide contrast; serve as a springboard for the new soloist; allow for the introduction of new material; serve as point of modulation; and provide points for changes of texture, mood, tempo, meter, etc.

Most of the same sources and materials which are used for introductions may also be used for interludes.

Patterns built on the various tension-producing scales (i.e., the diminished scale) make nice material for interludes. Fragments which were formerly background material often can be utilized for interludes.

Endings also draw on the same sources and materials as introductions and interludes. However, material must be introduced to slow the motion of a composition if the ending is to be successful.

A rather effective if somewhat cliched technique is to use exactly the same ending as introduction.

Recordings:

Lima Beba Samba from *R.S.V.P.* (Laurel Record LR-504) David Baker's 21st Century Bebop Band

Jeanne Marie At the Picture Show from *R.S.V.P.* (Laurel Record LR-504) David Baker's 21st Century Bebop Band

PaDoSpe from *Struttin'* (Laurel Record LR-505) David Baker's 21st Century Bebop Band

LoRob from *Struttin'* (Laurel Record LR-505) David Baker's 21st Century Bebop Band

Another technique is that of repetition of the final phrase. This might mean the melodic or harmonic phrase. **(example 1)**

Stretching the final phrase via a tag or a turnback is also quite useful. There are a number of standard turnbacks (see "turnback" chapter) and tags which are virtually public domain. **(example 2)**

Repetition of introductory or interlude material can be most attractive if used sparingly.

Abrupt endings **(example 3)**, fadeaways **(example 4)**, and special effects **(example 5)** are also useful if used judiciously.

Backgrounds should be used sparingly because they tend to inhibit the jazz soloist. The background instrumentation should contrast the soloist (i.e., brass soloist vs. reed background or a voicing that is reed heavy). The background should not stay in the comfortable register of the soloist. If the solo instrument and the background instrument are in the same comfortable range, obtain contrast by using other devices, (i.e., punch backgrounds, muted unisons, wide open voicings, etc.) Variations of the same background may be used. Avoid the exact repetition of an idea.

Before the sketch of the arrangement is made, countermelodies or secondary melodies must be dealt with. In most compositions, but particularly in compositions where tonal resources and instrumental forces are limited, secondary melodies must be classified and dispensed with. In general, melodies fall into two classes:
1. Main melodies
2. Subordinate melodies which include:
   a. Bass parts
   b. Countermelodies
   c. Inside parts
   d. Accompaniment parts
   e. Embellishing-type material

Bass parts should be carefully written, interesting to listen to and play. A countermelody is subordinate only to the main theme in importance. It does not usually have autonomy. It should sound good with all other parts, contrast the main melody, be idiomatic for the instrument to which it is assigned, and be scored in such a way as to not interfere with the forward thrust of the main melody.

Inside parts are usually rhythmic and harmonic rather than melodic. They support the main melody.

Accompaniment parts support the main melody and are essentially rhythmic rather than melodic.

Embellishing-type material might include riffs, fragments of the theme, and melodies based on the harmony or rhythm of the tune.

In making the actual sketch—don't forget—**work** for contrast. If the melody is in a single instrument, back it up with harmony parts in the other instruments. If the A section of a tune is scored for brass, then score B for woodwinds; if A is loud make B soft. **Always** work for **contrast.**

Every transition from one order to another—number of parts, type of scoring, change of mood, etc.,—should coincide with the introduction of a new idea, theme or phrase.

Modulations for the sake of modulation should be avoided. The technique of modulation in a jazz composition of normal length is so cliched as to warrant avoiding it entirely. However, in pop tunes and behind vocalists, it still can be used effectively.

One other thing should be attended to in order to make your arrangement effective and exciting: the "shout" chorus. The "shout" chorus is either the penultimate chorus or the final chorus of an arrangement or composition. In comparison with the rest of the arrangement the "shout" chorus is usually:

1. Louder
2. Much more active rhythmically.
3. Heavy on tutti ensemble writing.
4. The point of greatest **arranged** density, intensity and complexity.
5. Somewhere between a half chorus and two choruses long.
6. Built on tune material or new material and often paraphrases the melody. Often the "shout" chorus emphasizes some aspect of the harmony or rhythm of the composition.

The purposes of the "shout" chorus are to provide a written climax to the arrangement of the theme and in general synthesize what has taken place in the arrangement. (Study the arrangements included in this book and other arrangements from other sources for examples of "shout" choruses.)

SUGGESTED READING . . .

The Professional Arranger Composer by Russ Carcia

Composing for the Jazz Orchestra by William Russo

Sounds and Scores by Henry Mancini

Jazz and Commercial Arranging. Volume I: Block Writing Techniques, Rhythm and Melody by Andrew Charlton and John M. De Vries

Jazz and Commercial Arranging. Volume II: Accompaniment and Harmony by Andrew Charlton and John M. De Vries

SUGGESTED LISTENING . . .

Listen to recordings featuring arrangements by any good arranger-composer.

SUGGESTED ASSIGNMENTS . . .

1. Listen to and diagram several arrangements from the suggested listening. Make charts of the basic formats used.
2. Write arrangements in all idioms observing the rules put forth in this chapter.
3. Experiment with different kinds of introductions, interludes and endings to the same composition.

Putting An Arrangement Together

138

Chapter XIX

CHORD SUBSTITUTIONS

Very often the jazz player will find it advisable to use a different set of chords than those suggested by a piece of sheet music or a recording. There can be many reasons for making such a decision, among them the following:

1. To relieve the monotony of endless repetitions of the same chord changes
2. To introduce tension into an otherwise static situation
3. To provide a better (stronger) bass line
4. To provide more challenging and interesting vertical structures on which to improvise
5. To make a tune easier or more difficult to play on
6. To change the harmonic texture, for example, simple to complex and vice versa

Sometimes the technique may involve nothing more than re-interpreting the given chords (as in example A), or consolidating changes (as in example B), or some other simple task.

Example A: Dmi_6 E_7 is really $B\emptyset_7$ E_7

Example B: C_7 C_{13} C_{11} $C_7{}^{(\flat 9)}$ when consolidated equals C_7

At other times the technique may involve a much more complex reordering that may change the entire thrust of a set of chords.

Non-contextual Substitutions

Non-contextual substitutions are substitutions that seem to work relatively independently of the musical context. Obviously, it is not possible to operate in a musical manner without considering the harmonic surroundings to some degree.

Major Chords (I): Non-contextual substitution possibilities

1. For the major chord substitute the minor seventh chord a minor third below the root of the chord, as in the following example:

CM_7 CM_6 = Ami_9 (vi)

2. For the major chord substitute the minor seventh chord a major third above the root of the chord, as in the following example:

CM_7 CM_6 = Emi_7 (III)

3. For the major chord substitute the dominant seventh with a raised eleventh a perfect fourth above the root of the chord, as in the following example:

CM_7 CM_6 = $F_7{}^{(+11)}$ (IV)

139

4. For the major chord substitute any other major chord.

Minor Chords (II): Non-contextual substitution possibilities

1. For the minor chord substitute its dominant seventh, the root of which will be a perfect fourth above the root of the minor seventh chord, as in the following example:

2. For the minor chord substitute the major chord a minor third above the root of the chord, as in the following example:

3. For the minor chord substitute the half diminished seventh chord a minor third below the root of the chord, as in the following example:

4. For the minor chord substitute the other minor seventh chords which have their roots in the same diminished chord and their accompanying resolutions, as in the following examples:

Dmi$_7$, Fmi$_7$, Abmi$_7$, and Bmi$_7$ all have their roots in the same diminished chord; therefore, the following substitutions for Dmi$_7$ are possible according to the preceding rule.

5. For the minor chord substitute the diminished chord of the same name as the minor seventh chord in question, as in the following example (you can also use any of the inversions of the diminished chord):

6. For the minor chord substitute any other minor seventh type chord.

7. For the minor chord substitute any dominant seventh type chord.

8. For the minor chord substitute any diminished type chord.

9. For the minor chord substitute any half diminished seventh chord (minor seventh with a flat 5).

140

Dominant Seventh Chords (V): Non-contextual substitution possibilities

1. For the dominant seventh chord substitute the minor seventh a perfect fourth below the root of the chord, as in the following example:

2. For the dominant seventh chord substitute the major chord a whole step below the root of the chord, as in the following example:

3. For the dominant seventh chord substitute the half diminished seventh chord a major third above the root of the chord, as in the following example:

4. For the dominant seventh chord substitute the other dominant seventh chords which have their roots in the same diminished chord and their accompanying minor seventh chords, as in the following examples:

G_7, Bb_7, Db_7, and E_7 all have their roots in the same diminished chord; therefore, the following substitutions for G_7 are possible according to the preceding rule.

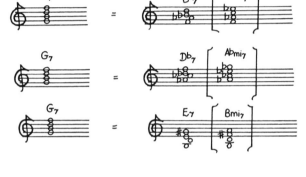

5. For the dominant seventh chord substitute the diminished chord a major third above the root of the chord, as in the following example (you can also use any of the inversions of the diminished chord):

6. For the dominant seventh chord substitute any other dominant seventh chord.

7. For the dominant seventh chord substitute any minor seventh chord.

8. For the dominant seventh chord substitute any diminished seventh chord.

9. For the dominant seventh chord substitute any half diminished seventh chord (minor seventh with a flat 5).

Contextual Substitutions

Contextual substitutions are substitutions which work only in specific contexts. In contextual substitutions a like or similar chord progression is presupposed if one is to use the substitutions given in the examples which follow. Additional examples of contextual substitutions can be found in chapter XX, The Blues, in the chart entitled "Blues Substitution Chart."

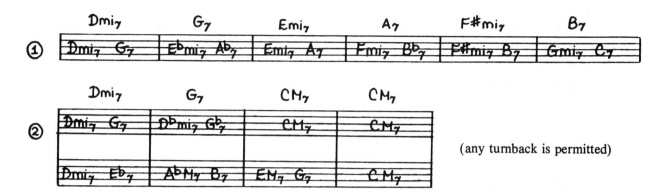

(any turnback is permitted)

The bottom line of example #2 is a set of changes known as the Coltrane changes. As can be readily discerned we can use these changes over a II/V$_7$/I progression that covers four measures, as in the following example:

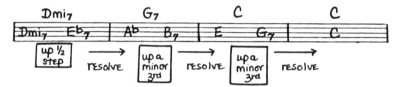

Note that the second chord (on beat three) of each measure is a dominant seventh which resolves to a major chord on beat one of measures 2, 3, and 4.

Example #3 is a chart illustrating a matrix which I evolved and developed based on the Coltrane changes.

Dmi$_7$	G$_7$	C	C
Dmi$_7$ E♭$_7$	A♭ B$_7$	E G$_7$	C
Dmi$_7$ B♭mi$_7$E♭$_7$	A♭ F♯mi$_7$B$_7$	E Dmi$_7$G$_7$	C
Dmi$_7$ G$_7$ B♭mi$_7$ E♭$_7$	A♭ Fmi$_7$ F♯mi$_7$ B$_7$	E C♯mi$_7$ Dmi$_7$ G$_7$	C
Fmi$_7$	B♭$_7$	E♭	E♭
Fmi$_7$ G♭$_7$	B D$_7$	G B♭$_7$	E♭
Fmi$_7$ D♭mi$_7$ G♭$_7$	B Ami$_7$ D$_7$	G Fmi$_7$ B♭$_7$	E♭
Fmi$_7$ B♭$_7$ D♭mi$_7$G♭$_7$	B G♯mi$_7$ Ami$_7$D$_7$	G Emi$_7$ Fmi$_7$B♭$_7$	E♭
A♭mi$_7$	D♭$_7$	G♭	G♭
A♭mi$_7$ A$_7$	D Cmi$_7$ F$_7$	B♭ D♭$_7$	G♭
A♭mi$_7$ Emi$_7$ A$_7$	D Cmi$_7$ F$_7$	B♭ A♭mi$_7$ D♭$_7$	G♭
A♭mi$_7$ D♭$_7$ Emi$_7$ A$_7$	D Bmi$_7$ Cmi$_7$ F$_7$	B♭ Gmi$_7$ A♭mi$_7$D♭$_7$	G♭
Bmi$_7$	E$_7$	A	A
Bmi$_7$ C$_7$	F A♭$_7$	D♭ E$_7$	A
Bmi$_7$ Gmi$_7$ C$_7$	F E♭mi$_7$ A♭$_7$	D♭ Bmi$_7$ E$_7$	A
Bmi$_7$ E$_7$ Gmi$_7$ C$_7$	F Dmi$_7$ E♭mi$_7$A♭$_7$	D♭ B♭mi$_7$ Bmi$_7$ E$_7$	A

142

Various chords can be altered in the chart, as in the following example:

Any chord in any column can be substituted for any other chord in the same vertical column, as in the following example:

For maximum variety memorize this chart with its combinatorial possibilities (which are astronomical!), such as in the following example:

Dmi_7 = D∅ or F or Bb (see substitutions for the minor 7th chord)

G_7 = $G_7^{(\#5)}$ or $G_7{}^{b9}_{b5}$ or $G_7{}^{\#9}_{\#5}$ or $G_7{}^{b9}_{\#5}$

C = Ami or A∅ or Gb

143

SUGGESTED READING . . .

The Lydian Chromatic Concept of Tonal Organization, pages 44-50, by George Russell
The Professional Arranger Composer by Russ Garcia
Jazz: An Introduction to Its Musical Basis (chapter 1) by Avril Dankworth
Techniques of Twentieth Century Composition (chapter 11) by Leon Dallin
Jazz Improvisation by David Baker
Advanced Improvisation by David Baker
The Schillinger System of Musical Composition, Volume I and II by Joseph Schillinger
Twentieth Century Music Idioms by G. Welton Marquis
Composing for the Jazz Orchestra by William Russo
Improvising Jazz by Jerry Coker
The Complete Method for Improvisation by Jerry Coker

SUGGESTED ASSIGNMENTS . . .

1. Know the reasons for using chord substitutions.
2. Know the principle of chord substitution.
3. Write substitutions for any ten standards.
4. Explain and exemplify contextual substitution.

Chapter XX

THE BLUES AND RHYTHM & BLUES

The term "blues" means to most jazz men a twelve measure structure of predetermined form. This form usually contains these basic chords arranged in this order.

$$I_7 \quad\quad IV_7 \quad\quad I_7 \quad\quad V_7 \quad\quad IV_7 \quad\quad I_7$$
$$\vdash 4 \dashv \quad \vdash 2 \dashv \quad \vdash 2 \dashv \quad //// \quad //// \quad \vdash 2 \dashv$$

This basic form is and has been used in one of its modifications by virtually every jazz man, rhythm & blues player, rock and roll, and country music player since before jazz began. Blues still comprises a large part of the modern jazz player's repertoire. It is an absolute necessity that the jazz writer be comfortable with the basic blues changes and its myriad variations.

Because of the unique nature of blues, this form demands special attention. There are a number of voicings, patterns, scales, cliches, etc., that are necessary tools for **all** writers.

One of the most popular blues voicings of modern writers follows: **(example 1)** It's a voicing that can be heard in the playing of most jazz pianists and of the writing of such diverse composer-arrangers as Quincy Jones, Gil Evans, George Russell and George Gershwin.

When using these voicings a thorough knowledge of the blues scale is mandatory if one is to handle accompanying melodies, interlude material, etc. (Refer to Chapter X.) Many times entire melody lines can be scored using just the blues voicing. (Interlude from *"The Professor"* follows.) **(example 2)**

The writer for reasons of variety or necessity (melodic) might deem it advisable on occasion to more rigidly structure or restructure the blues. The first step in the restructuring might be the change to the II V_7 progression in measures nine and ten rather than the V to IV chord. Now the player should use all of the knowledge he has concerning II V_7 progressions. The next step toward restructuring might take place in the eleventh and twelfth measures with the inclusion of some form of turnback, i.e., I bIII bVI bV, etc. **(example 3)**

For different harmonic approaches to the blues, see the chart on pages 151-152. For different material to be used in realizing the blues changes consult *Improvisational Patterns: The Blues* by David Baker.

Dat Dere	Bobby Timmons
Dis Heah	Bobby Timmons
Down Home	Curtis Fuller
In Walked Horace	J. J. Johnson
Mercy Mercy Mercy	Joe Zawinul
Politely	Bill Hardman
Sack O' Woe	Cannonball Adderley
Sister Sadie	Horace Silver
Sonnymoon for Two	Sonny Rollins
Work Song	Nat Adderley

Rhythm & blues tunes, while not always blues, embrace the spirit and general feeling normally connected with the blues. Most of these tunes have some basic points of agreement that set them apart from tunes of another genre. Some common points are:

1. Ostinato bass line. **(example 4)**
2. Generally relatively uncomplicated changes. **(example 5)**
3. Extensive use of the blues scale. **(example 6)**
4. Short riffs, melodic background patterns. **(example 7)**
5. Rhythmic priority with melody and harmony becoming secondary considerations. (Two and three levels of rhythmic activity.) **(example 8)**
6. Often vamps are interspersed. **(example 9)**
7. Very stylized. Usually adheres to one of the dance types current or otherwise. (i.e., Boogaloo, Funky Chicken, Yoke, Twist, Popcorn, Four Corners, etc.) **(example 10)**
8. Although the music is often perceived as listening music it is always conceived as "gebrauchsmusik."
9. Although the tunes will have different names all of the compositions of the same genre (boogaloo, twist, etc.) will have the same ᵃsic rhythm pattern (at least in bass and drums).

10. More often than not the electric bass is a part of the instrumental combination because of its facility and volume capabilities.
11. Often the climax to such tunes is achieved through the accumulation of short riff patterns stacked one on the other. **(example 11)**

SUGGESTED LISTENING . . .

Any recording by James Brown

Any of the Atlantic recordings of Aretha Franklin

Virtually any recording by Cannonball Adderley, Horace Silver, Jimmy Smith et al

SUGGESTED ASSIGNMENTS . . .

1. Listen to arrangements of blues of all types.
2. Write arrangements of several blues in the jazz idiom for different combinations of instruments. Also, try using some of the substitute changes listed.
3. Write some arrangements in the rhythm & blues idiom.

Blues and Rhythm & Blues

Although the G7 chord blankets the whole area, each melody note is harmonized using a different dominant 7th blues voicing.

149

BLUES SUBSTITUTION CHART

1	2	3	4	5	6	7	8	9	10	11	12
F7	F7	F7	F7	Bb7	Bb7	F7	F7	C7	Bb7	F7	F7
F7	Bb7	F7	Cmi F7	Bb7	Bo7	F7	D7	G7	C7	F7 Bb7	F7
						Cmi7 F7	Ami7 D7	Dmi7 G7	Gmi7 C7		
F7	Eb7	Db7	Cb7	BbM7	Bmi7 Eb7	Ami7 D7	Abmi7 Db7	Gmi7	C7	F7 D7	G7 C7
F7	G7	A7	B7	BbM7	Bmi7 E7	AM7	Bbmi7 Eb7	AbM7	Gmi7 C7	F7 D7	Db7 Gb7
F7	Bb7	Ami7 Gmi7	F#mi7 B7	Bb7	Bb7	F7 E7	Eb7 D7	Gmi7	F7	F7 D7	Db7 C7
FM7	Emi7 A7	Dmi7 G7	Cmi7 F7	Bb7 Ab7	Db E7	A C7	F7	Gmi7 C7	Dbmi7 Gb7	F Ab7	Db Gb7
F	F#o7 Gmi7 Abmi7	Ami7 D7	Cmi7 F7	Bb7	Ab7	Gb7	F7	Gmi7 C7	Bbmi7 Eb7	F7 Ab7	G7 Gb7
FM7	EbM7	DbM7	CbM7	Fmi7	Bb7	Emi7 A7	Ebmi7 Ab7	Dmi7 G7	Dbmi7 Gb7	F7 Eb7	Db7 C7
FM7	GM7	AM7	BM7	Bb7	E7	F Gmi7	Ami7 Abmi7	Gmi7	Gb7	F Ab	B D
F#o7 B7	E7 A7	D7 G7	C7 F7	Bb7	A7	Ab7	G7	C7	Bb7	F D	B Ab
FM7	Cmi7 Db7	Gb7 A7	D F7	B7 Bb7	Eb7 Ab7	Db7 Gb7	B7 E7	A7 D7	G7 C7	F7 Eb7	Db7 Gb7
F7	Eb7	F7	Eb7	BbM7	Bbmi7 Eb7	Ami7 D7	Gmi7 Ab7	Db E7	A7 C7	A7 D7	G7 C7

	1	2	3	4	5	6	7	8	9	10	11	12
	F7	Bb7	Cmi7 F7	F#mi7 B7	Bb7	Bb7	F7 Eb7	Db7	C7 Db7	C7	F7	Eb7
	F7 F#7	F7 F#7	F7 F#7	F7 F#7	Bb7 B7	Bb7 B7	F7 F#7	F7 F#7	C7 Db7	Bb7 B7	F7 F#7	F7
	FM7	Emi7 Ebmi7	Dmi7 Dbmi7	Cmi7 Bmi7	Bb M7	Bbmi7 Eb7	Emi7 A7	Abmi7 Db7	Dmi7 G7	Gmi7 C7	F7 Bb7	B7 Gb7
	F7	Ab7	B7	D7	Bb	Db7 Gb7	F7	F7	Dbmi7	Gb7	F7	F7
	F7	D7	B7	Ab7	Bb7							

All chords in the same column are interchangeable.

Chapter XXI

A MODEL ARRANGEMENT

153

154

Composition: JEANNE MARIE AT THE PICTURE SHOW

Arranger-Composer: DAVID N. BAKER

Page THREE

155

Composition: JEANNE MARIE AT THE PICTURE SHOW

Arranger-Composer: DAVID N. BAKER

Page FOUR

156

Composition: JEANNE MARIE AT THE PICTURE SHOW

Arranger-Composer: DAVID N. BAKER

157

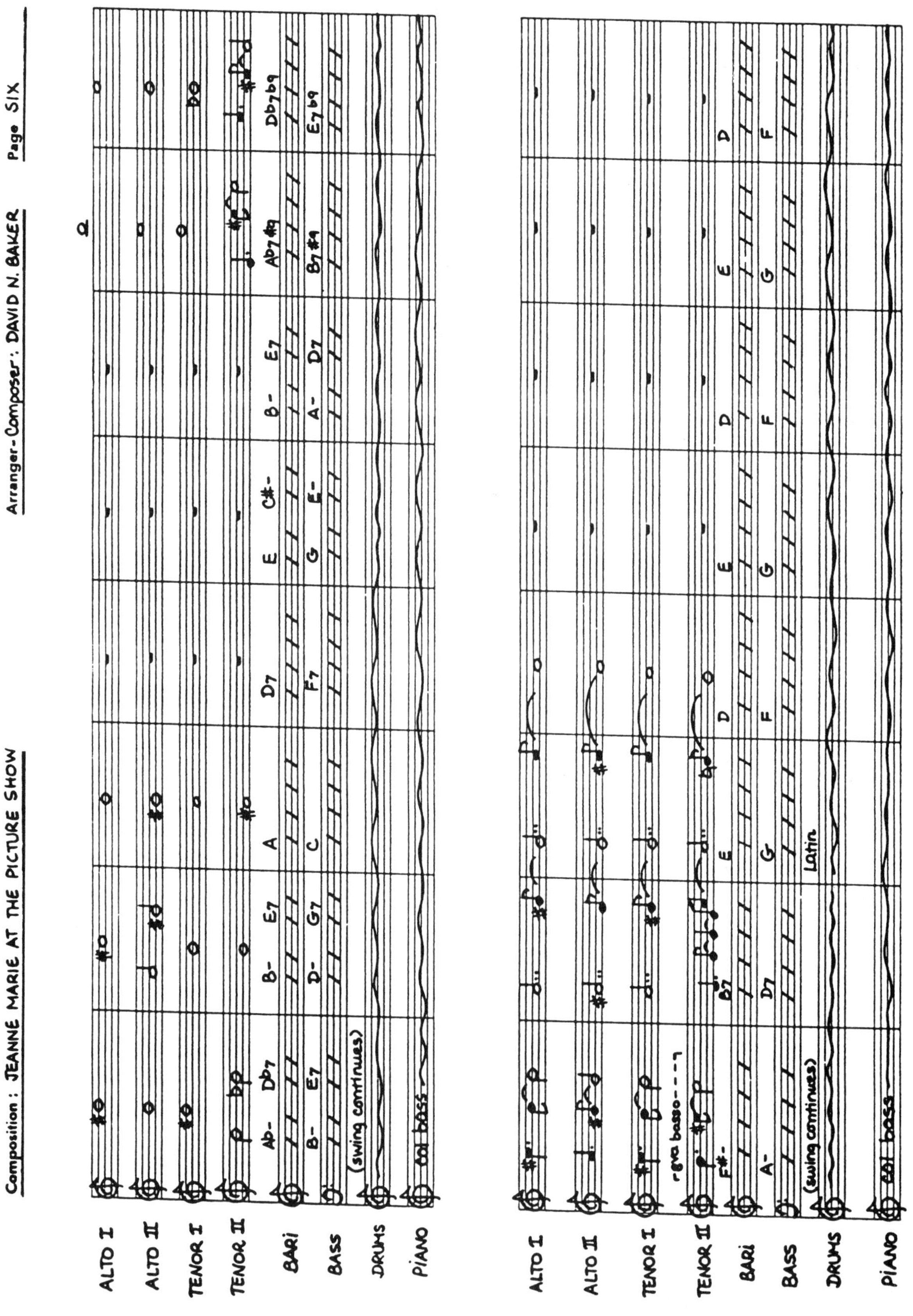

Composition: JEANNE MARIE AT THE PICTURE SHOW
Arranger-Composer: DAVID N. BAKER
Page SIX
ALTO I
ALTO II
TENOR I
TENOR II
BARI
BASS
DRUMS
PIANO
Ab- Db7
B- E7
A
D7
E C#-
B- E7
Ab7#9
Db7b9
B- E7
D- G7
C
F7
G E-
A- D7
B7#9
E7b9
(swing continues)
col bass
8va basso
F#-
B7
E
D
E
D
E
D
A-
D7
G
F
G
F
G
F
Latin
(swing continues)
col bass

Composition : JEANNE MARIE AT THE PICTURE SHOW

Arranger-Composer : DAVID N. BAKER

Page SEVEN

159

Composition: JEANNE MARIE AT THE PICTURE SHOW

Arranger-Composer: DAVID N. BAKER

Page EIGHT

160

Composition: JEANNE MARIE AT THE PICTURE SHOW
Arranger-Composer: DAVID N. BAKER
Page NINE
ALTO I
ALTO II
TENOR I
TENOR II
BARi
BASS
DRUMS
PiANO
(swing continues)
col bass
I
Latin
J
Solo
(Latin continues)
Swing
col bass

System 1

Instrument									
ALTO I	E	C#–	F#–	B7	Ab–	Db7	B–	E7	A	D7	E	C#–	F#–	B7
ALTO II											
TENOR I											
TENOR II											
BARI	G	E–	A–	D7	B–	E7	D–	G7	C	F7	G	E–	A–	D7
BASS				(swing continues)						
DRUMS										
PIANO	col bass									

System 2

Instrument									
ALTO I	B–	E7	A	Ab–	Db7	Gb	E–	A7	D	C#ø	F#7
ALTO II	mp									
TENOR I	mp									
TENOR II	col tenor I									
BARI										
BASS	D–	G7	C	B–	E7	A	G–	C7	F	Eø	A7
DRUMS			(swing continues)							
PIANO	col bass									

Composition : JEANNE MARIE AT THE PICTURE SHOW

Arranger-Composer : DAVID N. BAKER

Composition: JEANNE MARIE AT THE PICTURE SHOW   Arranger-Composer: DAVID N. BAKER   Page TWELVE

Composition : JEANNE MARIE AT THE PICTURE SHOW

Arranger-Composer : DAVID N. BAKER

Composition: JEANNE MARIE AT THE PICTURE SHOW   Arranger-Composer: DAVID N. BAKER   Page FOURTEEN

Composition: JEANNE MARIE AT THE PICTURE SHOW

Arranger-Composer: DAVID N. BAKER

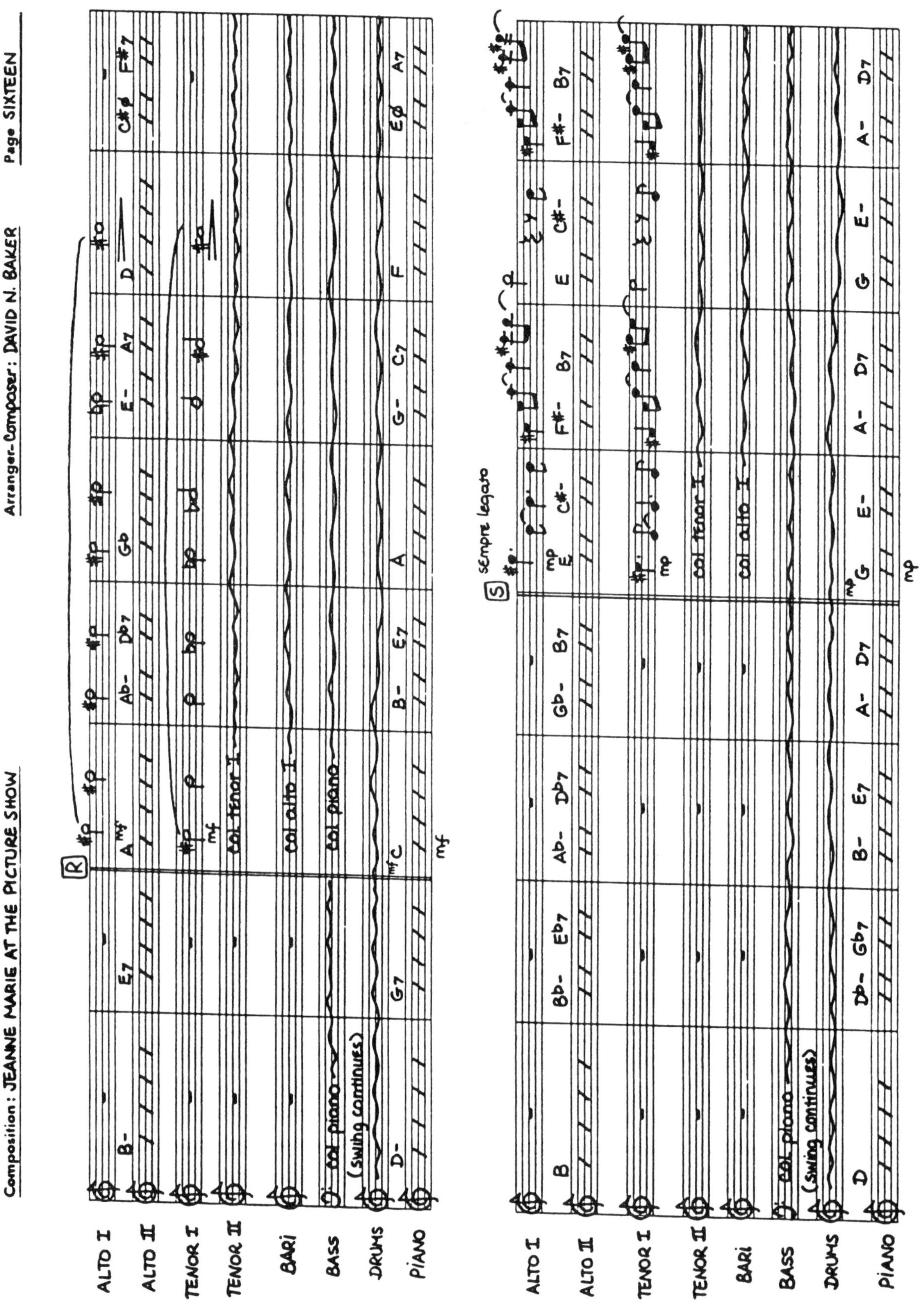
Composition: JEANNE MARIE AT THE PICTURE SHOW
Arranger-Composer: DAVID N. BAKER
Page SIXTEEN
ALTO I
ALTO II
TENOR I
TENOR II
BARI
BASS
DRUMS
PIANO
R
col tenor I
col alto I
col piano
(swing continues)
S
sempre legato
col tenor I
col alto I
col piano
(swing continues)

Composition: JEANNE MARIE AT THE PICTURE SHOW

Arranger-Composer: DAVID N. BAKER

Composition : JEANNE MARIE AT THE PICTURE SHOW

Arranger-Composer : DAVID N. BAKER

Page EIGHTEEN

170